WITHDRAWN

ROWAN'S PROGRESS

ROWAN'S PROGRESS

JAMES MCCONKEY

PANTHEON BOOKS, NEW YORK

Library of Congress Cataloging-in-Publication Data

McConkey, James.
Rowan's progress/James McConkey.
p. cm.
ISBN 0-679-40882-7
1. Rowan County (Ky.)—Social life and customs.
2. Rowan County (Ky.)—Biography.
3. McConkey, James—
Homes and haunts—Kentucky—Rowan County.
I. Title. F457.R7M36 1992
976.9′57—dc20   91-21248

Book Design By Fearn Cutler
Manufactured in the United States of America
First Edition

CONTENTS

A DREAM

The genesis of this book was a dream. In that dream, I was reenacting a moment in a doctor's office that took place about thirty-five years ago, while my wife, Jean, and I were young parents, living in a little town in the hills of eastern Kentucky. Our three-year-old son Larry was seated on a table under a bright lamp; his upper lip was badly split. He was grave before his injury, trying not to cry. "If I don't align the lip just right, the mend will show the rest of his life," the doctor said, in that gentle hill drawl that to an outsider suggests tolerance, an ironic control of self based on the acceptance of whatever life can bring. But her hand was shaking so much that she asked Jean to hold it as she began to stitch.

The dream faded, to be replaced, as I was awakening, by a momentary but very clear image of the face of my son as he looked now, at age thirty-eight. His lip was perfectly aligned, unblemished by a scar. Indeed, so carefully had the doctor sutured the lip that the wound —inflicted by a tooth or claw of an overexcited cocker spaniel puppy as Larry was romping about the house with him—had been lost to my conscious mind for maybe a quarter century.

The professional name of that doctor—the one on

her office door and in the slender telephone directory for Morehead, then an isolated town of about three thousand inhabitants in the Cumberland (now Daniel Boone) National Forest—was C. Louise Caudill, M.D. The initial stood for "Claire," but to her patients she was "Dr. Louise." Throughout the six years—from the fall of 1950 until the fall of 1956—that my family remained in that town, Dr. Louise treated not only Larry but our second child Cris, who had been born in a hospital in Lexington, since there was no such facility in Morehead then.

In those years, the town (despite the presence of the small state college where I held my first real teaching position) had but two doctors active enough that I knew of their presence. Dr. Louise had an extraordinarily heavy work load; she and her assistant—a nurse known to everybody as Susie—attended to patients throughout the county, often delivering babies in remote cabins in the hills, sometimes being gone for two or three days. Word spread rapidly when Dr. Louise and Susie returned from the countryside; hill and townspeople not too sick to require home care, some of them men but most of them women and children, would line the staircase to her second-story office, above a jewelry store on Main Street, waiting for them to show up—and so Dr. Louise and Susie had to tend to them, before getting any sleep. On the evening that Dr. Louise sewed up Larry's lip, she had been without sleep for three days; fatigue was the reason that she needed my wife to steady her hand as she worked. For some reason I don't recall, Susie wasn't there.

What had caused me to dream about such a distant event? With the birth of each child, a parent is born to a new and immediate concern or apprehension, for life seems a precious but delicate affair, and each infant breath a kind of small miracle; the worry about possible accidents or illnesses, about all the unknown vagaries waiting for the moment they become fixed as part of a child's destiny, remains with the parent long after the child is grown and gone far from home—remains, indeed, until the father or mother loses memory to his or her death or disease. Still, no fear for a child had been attached to this particular dream, not even as I relived the sight of the doctor's trembling hand; in fact, so quickly had the image of my son as an adult followed the episode that it seemed I had dreamed of the gash and then of the doctor's sewing of it so that I could juxtapose them against a picture of the unblemished face of my oldest son that was sharper than any willed recollection of it has ever permitted me.

The dream and succeeding image seemed gratuitous. As an affirmation—of healing; of the power of human hands, whatever the fallibility of our mortal condition—they might have constituted one of those blessings of memory that are effortlessly released from their deep burial to offset a much different kind of double vision in our later years. Our youthful ambitions, directed as they are on rising in the world, tend to take that world and all of its institutions—universities, corporations, nations—with their surrounding rules and values and promised awards as a solid given. But as we gradually detach ourselves from the occupation that has been part of our social identity, a certain uneasiness sets in. At vulnerable moments our individual lives, and even the history of our species, are held up to a dispassionate ideal or ultimate meaning so far beyond human achievement, or even formulation in language, that the competitive and frequently violent sociopolitical world in which we have struggled for recognition or status becomes as petty as it is illusory.

At any rate, I had been granted a fine dream, one that acknowledged the competence and caring of a doctor, a woman fully engaged in matters of everyday life, whose qualities, though remarkable for their separation from convention, egoism, or professional pose, I indeed had been in the process of forgetting.

===

Soon after my family's arrival in Morehead, Larry, still a baby, developed a slight fever. At the suggestion of a new acquaintance, Jean and I took him to see Dr. Louise. We took our place on the bottom step of the staircase that augmented the small waiting area, moving upward, step by democratic step (nobody being summoned ahead of anybody else), until it was our turn to enter a room with a bare wooden floor, a table and some chairs, and an elderly couch. At first we confused Susie the nurse, who was a fairly tall and slender young woman, with the doctor, since Susie was the one wearing a white smock. Maybe Dr. Louise had been too busy to don her own uniform, or for some reason had discarded it. In any event, she was wearing jeans and a sweatshirt. Though smaller than Susie—she wasn't much more than five feet tall—she too was slender, and her eyes showed a friendly and youthful vitality.

"Well, what's bothering the young-un?" she asked, gently taking Larry into her arms. After we told her all that we knew, and while she was making the customary investigations with thermometer and stethoscope and tongue depressor and mirrors, she made small talk with us, asking us (as best I can recollect) such questions as how did we like the little town and where had we come from (our accents gave us away as Northerners). She said she knew where we'd bought a house, and so on. "Well, the symptoms don't add up to anything that makes sense to me," she said cheerfully, giving Larry a last little thump or pat on his back. "Let's sit down together and see what the book says."

So Jean, with Larry on her lap, and I dutifully sat on the old couch, with Dr. Louise between us. She turned the pages of her big medical text (which categorized diseases under identifiable common features, in the manner of a Peterson bird or tree guide) until we found a disease that perfectly fit the symptoms. I've forgotten now the name of the ailment, which wasn't serious (given medication, Larry quickly recovered) but not

Dr. Louise's forthright admission that she didn't know everything already, nor her willingness to include Jean and me in the search through a textbook. A couple of years later, on Dr. Louise's advice, we took Larry to a Lexington specialist to see about a hearing problem in one ear. The specialist told us that, among the physicians in Lexington, our doctor had a reputation as a rural practitioner who had never been known to make an incorrect diagnosis. Jean and I, who already trusted her, found his testimony, while gratifying, far less surprising than the openness that had at once won our confidence in her.

On the day before we left Morehead for upstate New York and my new teaching position at Cornell, Dr. Louise, busy though she always was, stopped at our house to have a final look at her two young patients, and to say good-bye to Jean and me. As she was standing at the doorway, she said to me, as frankly as ever, "I always figured you would leave."

"Why did you think that?" I asked, surprised.

"Because you're too good for this place," she said, with a sweep of her arm large enough to include everything—the surrounding hills as well as the town itself —to which she had dedicated herself and of which she was a part. After a firm handshake, she briskly walked out of our lives.

I remembered that remark on the morning of my dream, not because I was flattered by it, but because of what I didn't say in response, though the thought

immediately came to my mind: *If I truly were good,
Louise, I'd stay here, as you do.* But actually I was glad to
be leaving a hill college with maybe eight hundred students for a major university in the East. Unlike Louise,
I had no commitments to a specific region. My friend-
ships were mainly with my colleagues, most of whom
had come from elsewhere, and with a few bright and
caring students. I'd never managed a successful conversation with any of those impoverished hill people
whom so much of her professional career was dedicated
to helping. I found them shy and proud, difficult if not
impossible for an outsider (maybe shy and proud himself) to know. Caught up in my college duties as well as
my aspirations, I had made little effort to absorb the
history or even the atmosphere of a county foreign to
much of what I believed myself to be. Only after I left
did I regret that I had permitted so much to slip by,
considering it merely quaint or picturesque. For
instance, I had never attentively listened to the ballad
singer who, blind and crippled by age, sat in a wheel-
chair outside the bus station, a cup for coins in his lap,
singing to passing and indifferent travelers the bloody
legends of Rowan County and the stories of love and
betrayal that were common to all Appalachia. Had the
instrument he plucked, strummed, or bowed been a
store-bought guitar or violin, or perhaps a home-
crafted dulcimer? I didn't even know that.

In my early years at Cornell, one of the chairmen of
my department was a native Kentuckian whose voice

(despite a Yale education and a professional lifetime in
the East) still contained a touch of drawl. Now and
then, he consciously emphasized the accent for humorous or satiric effect. I had a recurrent dream in which
that drawl became sardonic, implicating me in a past he
knew about but had outdistanced. "Na-ow, Jim," he
would say to me, "don't you think you ought to take
yo'self ri-i-uht back to *Mo*-hay-ed?" "Of course, Bill,"
I would reply after some hesitation, and would wake in
terror to a Morehead I had never known, a dark cell in
the prison of my past to which my inadequacies had
sentenced me. On one particular night, though, when
he came to me with that question, my answer while the
same was immediate and made with a chuckle that
turned into laughter—for the dream was now a joke at
his expense, and Morehead a place of infinite promise
and delight, a bit of geography in my future that was
far superior to everything in the present he wanted to
exile me from.

And so my latest Morehead dream, in which my
subconscious mind had faithfully reconstructed an
actual experience, had caused me to remember, among
other things, my first Morehead dreams, and to see
them as the psychical projections that they were; and to
realize how much and how long a town and its county
had existed for me, not as a geographical entity with
living inhabitants that included an actual C. Louise Caudill, M.D., but as a symbol by which I consciously or
unconsciously judged my professional competence and

standing. I now felt my Kentucky past to have been a
swift journey down the subterranean river of a lime-
stone cave, the lantern in the prow of the little barge
that carried me along only now and then glowing upon
glittering formations or illuminating side passages never
to be explored.

As a man of sixty-six, troubled by the solipsistic
myopia of his youth and worried that a new ailment,
self-diagnosed as double vision, might be interfering
with his current notions of reality, I immediately sat
down and wrote a long letter to Dr. Louise. I told her
many of the things I have put down here, and said that
I would like very much to see her and Susie, and hoped
that the pair of them would remember Jean and me
enough to welcome a visit from us sometime. Did you
ever get that clinic you wanted? I asked, recalling her
desire for a clean and comfortable place in town where
the pregnant hill women could come for safe delivery
of their babies. I wrote all that, not knowing whether
Dr. Louise and her nurse were still in practice; not
knowing, even, if they were alive. I wrote the letter
because it made me happy to do so, not because I
expected a reply.

2

I wrote that letter in early October. In January, Jean and
I planned to fly to Florida for a brief visit with her sister

and brother-in-law before taking another flight to the Yucatan peninsula. But, because of a phone call I received about a month after my letter to Dr. Louise, we ended up driving to Florida in order to spend a couple of days in Morehead *en route*.

When I answered the phone late one evening, the caller said, "This is Susie, Jim."

"Susie?" Among my friends and acquaintances were any number of Susies: former students, present and past colleagues, country neighbors. "Oh, *Susie*," I cried, only then connecting the name with the soft eastern Kentucky accent that had given me an immediate and surprising nostalgia.

"Louise isn't much at writing letters, but she wants you to know that she surely did appreciate yours; and so did I."

"Is Louise all right?" The thought struck me that maybe she had been incapacitated by an illness, maybe a stroke; after all, she would be in her seventies.

"Why, she's just fine, fine as ever. She's sitting here by me, at the kitchen table." In the pause that followed, I heard a muffled chuckle, no doubt from Louise herself. "She's been after me to write you, but I'm not one to spell out my heart in letters either. We were wasting time just now wondering what you and Jean were up to, and what had happened to the babies—"

"Babies?"

"Larry and Cris. The ones we used to doctor. So I just picked up the phone and dialed your number; and here I am to tell you we'd be delighted to see you, as soon as you can get yourselves down here. Here's Louise."

"Jim?"

"Louise?"

"If you think it would be fun to see us, come right on down; it would be just as much fun for us to have you." Her voice was a bit deeper than Susie's, and more measured or deliberate; it was the voice of my dream, the drawl that seemed amused or playful while remaining in control, able to cope. "Come on a weekday before five or so, you can stop at the office, right on Main Street."

"You're still practicing?"

"Shoot! How else would I pass the time, except for a little swimming or tennis when the sun shines? Later than five, or on weekends, give us a call from town for directions to the house. It's a little peculiar, getting here."

"Wouldn't it be easier if we stayed at the Midland Trail?" I remembered that to be the name of the two-story brick hotel on Main Street; highway 60, which ran through town, had been built on the old wilderness trail.

"You'd find that just a mite uncomfortable. The beds are all gone. It went out of business after the interstate bypassed the town."

"What interstate?"

Louise laughed. "You won't recognize the place,

Jim. The changes have come so fast, oldtimers like Susie and me hardly know what to make of it."

"But you said your office was on Main Street. That's not one of the changes, then? You're still above the jewelry store that's next to the pool hall?" My real question, of course, was whether or not she had been able to get the clinic, that dream of hers. Understanding what I meant, Louise said her office was now in the clinic, constructed according to her own plans, that was about a block away from the former office, but that it had been built so many years ago it had outlived its usefulness as a little lying-in hospital for the country women.

Like our bodies, towns are apt to change considerably in thirty-five years, but voices don't. Talking with Louise and Susie, I was hearing voices indistinguishable from those I remembered and, of course, seeing both the doctor and the nurse (as they would be seeing Jean and me) as still young. The telephone call, then, seemed a transmission from a distant time as well as a distant place. No doubt this was one of the reasons (another was my subconscious idea of the stopover as a return to the past) that, despite Louise's cautionary words, I was to be bewildered and disoriented by Morehead's transformation.

In the 1950s, Morehead, small though it was, had been a congested community, so confined by its valley that houses seemed to press against each other. A two-lane asphalt highway bisected the town, connecting it (seventy twisting miles to the west) to Lexington; and (roughly as many tortuous miles to the east) to Ashland and neighboring Huntington, West Virginia. Its only wide street was the boulevard, with its scattering of college buildings, that looped from the business district back to Main Street, meeting it at the town's edge. The few residential streets resembled paved alleys, and were apt to end in dirt trails that wound their way alongside seasonal streams, up the forested hollows.

===

An efficient four-cylinder engine creates a white noise conducive to the form of reverie that recovers old emotions, lost sensations. At about the midpoint of Jean's and my fourteen-hour drive, I found myself recapturing wisps or fragrances of what it had felt like to be a young man in the town toward which we were headed. Dusk came before we crossed the Big Sandy River, that natural boundary between West Virginia and Kentucky. Jean was driving. When freed from any willed effort at recall, our memories can select details from a present environment that will encompass an entire past. For me, the headlights of our little Plymouth Horizon became other headlights shining through fog, and the glowing radio dial in the dashboard a similar one in our Morehead living room; and these two images expanded to create much of the atmosphere, as subjective as it was enveloping, within which I had once lived.

Though I had often driven through mists or heavy

fog in Morehead, that particular memory of headlights beaming into fog came from an experience on our first Christmas Eve in town. I had forgotten to buy a stand for our tree; the telephone operator (I had already learned she was the one to call in any emergency, however large or small: a comforting night-time intelligence, she was privy enough to whatever was going on in town to transfer long-distance calls to the house in which the desired recipient was playing bridge) told me that the Big Store on Railroad Street might have a few, and that it was still open. The valley fog was particularly thick that night; I had difficulty finding the side street that led toward the railroad tracks. As I came out of the Big Store (called that because it sold appliances and furniture as well as clothing, yard goods, and seasonal items, all in a friendly confusion) with my purchase, I heard what seemed to be drunken curses, and then a single explosion, as if a gun had been fired; but the fog muffled sound so that I couldn't be certain. Back in my car, I switched on the lights, twin tunnels that dimly lit the point at which they met, and backed the car in an arc so that I could make out a good stretch of what seemed to be empty sidewalk and deserted buildings.

Christmas Eve in Morehead, Kentucky, I said to myself. I said nothing to Jean, as we decorated the tree, about what might have been only my imagination; after all, Railroad Street, which contained a number of wooden stores with false façades that made it look like the set of a Western movie, encouraged fantasies of cowardly snipers and shootouts. Furthermore, though the town was dry, there was a saloon on Railroad Street to lend credence to the set; it was common knowledge that a bootlegger sold whiskey by the glass as well as by the bottle behind the shuttered windows of one of those false-fronted structures.

But the sounds had been authentic. In the next issue of the weekly Rowan County *News,* I read a brief item about the jailing of a male who, on Christmas Eve, allegedly had killed another male on that street, following an argument in the saloon. Naturally, I followed the case in the ensuing newspaper accounts. Because both the alleged killer and his victim had many kinfolk in the region, there was difficulty in obtaining either a jury or a conviction. Ultimately, the charge was changed to a much smaller offense and the defendant spent a few months behind bars. Because of adverse publicity, the bootlegger was forced out of business, at least at that location.

The lightness of the punishment struck me as strange, as did the treatment of the bootlegger, who hadn't been charged at all. For that matter, the local option law, which, like Prohibition, spawned any number of bootleggers (a profession that I thought had been rendered superfluous in my childhood with the repeal of the Eighteenth Amendment), was alien to my experiences. Throughout our stay in Morehead, I felt uneasy to be attending parties at which the host, having run

out of beverages, called the mayor or the sheriff to discover where supplies could be purchased on that particular night. I never found out why our elected officials
did this; maybe they were simply paying a necessary
obeisance to, or arranging an expedient compromise
with, that fierce Appalachian independence that makes
lawmakers and law enforcers suspect.

Still, the community at large (urged on, I came to
understand, by clergy and bootleggers alike) had voted
to keep the county dry. Supporters of local option
included a majority of the veteran teachers at the college, most of whom had been born in the region. A
recently appointed college president who had come
from Nashville—during my brief tenure, there were
three presidents, the other two Kentucky natives—once
paid a call to my office to make sure I would attend, as
what he hoped would be a moderating influence, an
emergency faculty meeting demanded of him by a co-
alition of older teachers. Its purpose was to determine
whether or not a graduate student, caught by the police
beneath a streetlight late one night while celebrating the
completion of his studies with a can of beer, had sufficient moral character to be awarded his master's degree
in education. After an angry debate and by a narrow
margin, the faculty decided not to withhold the degree.

Meanwhile, I was becoming friendly with the owner
of the Oldsmobile agency. I got my gasoline from the
pumps in front of his showroom, and on frequent evenings chatted with him from a chair adjoining his desk.

He was a tolerant man, generous in his sympathies, and his political attitudes were congenial with mine; ours was one of those relationships that are nurtured by banter. Once I asked him how it could be that Kentucky, famous for its bourbon, its beautiful women, and its fast horses, could include an enclave like Rowan County, which, while it might have its share of pretty girls, had mules but not a single horse I knew of, and had outlawed whiskey. He said he knew a man out toward Salt Lick who long ago had bought a fine little saddle mare, and maybe old Sim still had old Molly in pasture. In speaking of the dry law, though, he became much more serious. It was something, he said, he had to defend. He did so by referring to a past era of open saloons that brought bloodshed. Alcohol, he instructed me, had a long history in this county and elsewhere in the mountains as the major stimulant to rivalry between families. But it was a subject he refused to expand upon, maybe because it touched upon his own ancestors (he was a member of one of the town's long-time families), or those of others he felt a loyalty toward.

We tend to remember remarks that imply far more than they reveal. I used to wonder if maybe the Christmas Eve violence hidden from my sight, its sounds muffled, had been a vestige of some old and bitter conflict between families. The subject of past feuding, though, was one that no native of the region seemed willing to discuss. In May of our last year in Morehead, the Rowan County *News,* in honor of the centenary of

the founding of the county, put out a huge edition—
108 pages—dealing chiefly with the past. One article
alone made a major, if tangential, reference to a feud
known as the Rowan County War; its actual subject was
an 1888 proposal by the state legislature to abolish the
county unless the feuding stopped. In a box, the newspaper's editor explained the reason for excluding the
feud from scrutiny, even at this late date:

> The Rowan County *News* has the story of all the grue-
> some and seemingly almost inhuman killings and deeds
> of the Rowan County War as historians compiled, and in
> many instances, magnified, the three years of the struggle
> in which citizens were afraid to walk on the streets or be
> out at night. Hundreds upon hundreds of present Rowan
> Countians are descendants of the Tollivers, Logans, and
> others who participated in the feud. Reprinting the story
> of the Rowan County War could mean only embarrass-
> ment for scores of our fine, progressive citizens of today
> and it is not the purpose of this edition to start any more
> feuds—to lay blame on any action—or to rehash a period
> in our history that is best forgotten. . . .

Surprisingly enough, that historical edition of the
Rowan County *News* contained in a prominent position
a two-column picture of one outsider to the region—
my wife, Jean. Some years earlier, she had been hired as
the college's one-person news bureau, as well as to teach
a course in journalism and serve as adviser to the student
newspaper; the editor of the county weekly had asked
her for help with the special issue. The caption to the

picture said that, in addition to writing articles about the centennial for the metropolitan papers, she "had penned much of the material" in the edition. Despite her contacts with businessmen and other established citizens, her only knowledge of a possible connection between past feuding and present families came from that little editorial box, which she and I read after the newspaper was published.

Had I persisted, I might have found on some undisturbed shelf of the college library enough documentary evidence to unlock a mystery that made me a stranger. I didn't; "gruesome and seemingly almost inhuman killings and deeds" had little to do with what I valued. I preferred to listen on our family radio to sounds of an opposing and more congenial culture, the music and informational programs from WQXR, the radio station of the *New York Times*.

The surrounding hills generally made for a fading and distorted reception of radio signals. A local station came into existence during our stay in Morehead, but it devoted its hours to gospel music and preachers whose excited utterances, punctuated by gasps for breath, were undecipherable to me. Through some topographical quirk, WQXR came through to us with greater strength and fidelity than even the local station did. I had discovered the phenomenon quite by chance; one night, as I was driving into the gravel patch at the end of our tiny yard, the car radio lost the wavering signals of the station it had been tuned to, maybe in Cincinnati or Wheeling; in its place, with a glorious resonance, came the chords of Beethoven's Ninth Symphony. I rushed into the house, to discover that our high-fidelity set (a valued possession, as one of the first of such sets in town: I had put it together from components ordered by mail from an Allied Radio Corporation catalog) caught the music as if the orchestra were in the living room, or at least as if WQXR, knowing we had tweeters as well as a woofer, was beaming a special signal to us.

The announcers I remember from those years were Pru Devon and Martin Bookspan. The former introduced a program sponsored by the Ritz Thrift Shop, purveyors of used fur coats, that was called "Nights in Latin America" and which we listened to while eating our supper; the latter was in charge of the following and much longer program of classical music, interspersed with ads for Sam Goody and others. We listened to Martin Bookspan's program after our children were in bed and Jean was writing her news stories while I graded another set of freshman themes.

From a radio in my upstate New York farmhouse, I once heard the voice of Pru Devon announcing musical selections for a Rochester public radio station; and occasionally I have heard Martin Bookspan as the unseen announcer for televised orchestral events on PBS. Hearing those voices has always filled me with a longing for my Morehead past, identical in kind to the longing I had then while listening to them on WQXR, and makes me realize how much our unobtainable desires impart a poignant value to where we are and what we presently possess.

On the night that WQXR increased its power from ten thousand to fifty thousand watts, our radio got nothing but static, whistles, and the competing noises of closer stations. No longer did those signals from Manhattan fortuitously bounce off some hill slope, to enter our living room as if Carnegie Hall, the Ritz Thrift Shop, and Sam Goody's various record stores all could be found up one neighboring hollow or another. Such a loss contributed to the dissatisfaction that led to our departure.

==

On the night of our return all those years later, we approached Morehead on a banked, gradually curving interstate highway that, although it afforded vista after vista of whitened and empty hills made spectral in starlight, did away with that old sense of separation so crucial to my remembered feelings. The headlights occasionally lit wisps of mist, and gave the luminescence of fireflies to exit signs for invisible towns and villages—Grayson, Sandy Hook, Olive Hill—that Jean and I knew from former Sunday drives on more primitive roads.

We were listening on the radio to a lovely quartet neither of us recognized. The radio signals were surprisingly clear. "Do you suppose we can get the Morehead station yet?" I asked, as the quartet came to an end. I was about to switch the dial when the announcer identified the performers as members of the Morehead University resident quartet, and the station itself as that of the university I had known as a tiny college. As we slowed for the Morehead exit, the station picked up a National Public Radio program, "Adventures in Good Music": the accents of Karl Haas followed, as infuriatingly affected or as amusingly campy as they were at home. "My God, can you imagine *that,*" I cried, clicking off the radio, not knowing if I were referring to Karl Haas, the Morehead resident quartet, or the neon signs for the liquor stores, the fast-food franchises, the video outlets, the Holiday Inn, and the shopping mall.

It was a town that had so thoroughly entered the mainstream of America that nobody could be truly lost in it unless he or she knew it from a previous epoch. (Stores selling liquor, beer, and wine were not the only indication that a past violence had been mastered. The next day I was to pick up from a placarded store rack a brochure about the Rowan County War, describing participants and killings in detail.) All that distinguished this community from any other small city in the land were two institutions at opposite ends of the downtown district: a university, complete with dormitory and library towers, a student union, laboratories, classroom structures, and a sports complex, at one end; at the other, a modern hospital, a seven-story building with wings and a large and illuminated parking lot—a facility much too extensive to serve only the immediate area, regardless of the town's growth.

Nothing was familiar to us, except for the eyes of Dr. Louise as she opened her door to our knock; they held the humorous and friendly glint I remembered, and all the old vitality. As yet, of course, I had no idea that this small and modest doctor had played a major role in the transformations that still were bewildering me, and had surmounted prejudices and rivalries that made a far greater barrier than mist-covered hills ever could; or that she (born Claire Louise Caudill, and a lifelong member of the local Christian church of her baptism) had been unofficially sainted for her efforts, as the St. Claire for whom the Catholic hospital had been named—an ecumenical honor so fitting to her nature and accomplishments that it made sainthood itself respectable in that resolutely non-Catholic region.

"Welcome back," she said. Susie was at her side. Jean and I entered; the four of us embraced. It was as if Jean and I, strangers in Morehead while living there, had returned to a home that always had been ours.

3

Of all the Mayan sites Jean and I visited in the Yucatan, Coba was the one I liked best. I was drawn to Coba because it is as remote as it is beautiful, because the pyramids are towering tumbles of stones from which only the immediate trees and undergrowth have been cleared, and because I found it a pleasure to greet small children of Mayan descent leading their pigs through the ruins, in search, not of stelae, but rooting grounds. Jean and I, in leaving the circuitous path for a vantage point in the tangle of vegetation, discovered that the trail had been worn into the surface of an ancient causeway or road maybe thirty feet wide, built four to six feet above ground level, and (whatever the natural obstacles) proceeding in a straight line. Coba is the hub for a number of such causeways, some of which extend for many miles, a prodigious engineering feat for purposes that remain an archaeological riddle.

During our explorations at Coba, we used a guidebook to find various ruins, but no guide. When a civilization is dead, one has the illusion of making contact with it through personal discoveries. And it gratified me that the stones had not been painstakingly reconstructed into immaculate pyramids, and that so many artifacts lay buried beneath their mounds. Any city long dead has disappeared into the mystery that envelops continuing life itself, and our imaginations respond most fully to ruins at which there has been a minimum of digging and Portland cement.

From our wonder at such ruins, what can we, the still living, reconstruct, both as a bulwark for our own imperiled civilization and as a help to the riddle of our personal existence? In the days following Jean's and my return to upstate New York, I found myself thinking less of a dead community in the Yucatan than of a still-growing one in eastern Kentucky and of the transformations that had come to it. Sequestered for generations, the town and its county had compressed into my lifetime much of the social and cultural history of our nation's last one hundred and fifty years. To return to that region after three decades was like viewing a living organism through time-lapse photography. The town's twin institutions—its modern university and its equally modern and well-staffed hospital—had given it sufficient pride in the present to enable it to come to terms with its past.

Education and medicine were intertwined and had made an immeasurable difference. Dr. Louise, who had been the chief driving force in the establishment of the hospital, had also been an agent in a long, educative process begun as an attempt to bring an end to the vendettas that had made the county notorious. I learned all this and much more during our stopover, not so much from Louise and Susie as from townspeople who were glad to talk with us about their community. One of them, an admirer of Louise, told me that the doctor was related to the family that his own family had warred against; another, whose ancestors included members on both sides of the conflict, said, "I dearly love Louise, and think of her as a spiritual descendant of Cora Wilson Stewart, whom my daddy worked for when she was superintendent of schools."

I knew as little about Cora Wilson Stewart as about the Rowan County War in the 1880s, or its aftermath.

Still, I was beginning to view Rowan County as a kind of living laboratory, a region of such rapid alteration, not only in institutions but in human attitudes, that the past was yesterday and the future possibly tomorrow. And I was beginning to see Dr. Louise not only as one who had affected me personally, but as one whose presence had affected many others in an equally benign way; as best I could tell, that diminutive, rural doctor was the most influential contemporary figure in the evolving history of her county.

Future archaeologists, I told myself, will never uncover stelae bearing Louise's image, for our monuments, like those of the ancient Mayans, honor political and military leaders. (Some of the stelae in Coba show a woman, but she is a ruler, her throne the submissive backs of kneeling captives taken in warfare, their hands bound.) Such monuments are of no help to anybody whose obsession it is to reinvest the human world with a meaning that transcends violence and brutal power.

At least one local truth I had gained from my years in Morehead is that eastern Kentuckians get a great part of their definition from the history of the region they were born into. What I now was beginning to realize was the degree to which Morehead and its surrounding territory (perhaps here like many places in America) had achieved *their* present definition through a historical progression in which the actions and even the attitudes of individuals—Louise and her predecessors—were supremely important.

THE PAST:
A WAR

1

In his *Little Kingdoms: The Counties of Kentucky, 1850–1891*, Robert M. Ireland, writing in 1971, remarks that Kentucky is second among the states in the union "in number of counties per square mile," a status that is the consequence of its nineteenth-century "proficiency in the art of creating counties, carving out 100 by 1850 and adding twenty more in the next sixty-two years."

The General Assembly of the Commonwealth formed Rowan County (pronounced by generations of its citizens as a single syllable, "round" without the "d") in 1856 from sections of Morgan and Fleming counties. It was named for Judge John T. Rowan, who, though he helped form the first constitution of the state and was a United States senator at the time of his death, is best known now as the proprietor of the estate in Bardstown that inspired Stephen Collins Foster to write "My Old Kentucky Home." The reason given by legislators for the creation of the county, Ireland says, was simply to provide a convenient county seat at Morehead (also named for a politician, Governor James T. Morehead) for the thousand or so residents of the new entity. Another historian suggests a second, more crassly political, reason—Rowan might have been formed in consequence of machinations in Fleming over the location

of its own county seat. Political considerations may
have been involved also in the attempt to abolish
Rowan County in 1888, following the last major conflict—a pitched battle in Morehead—of the Rowan
County War, sometimes referred to as the Martin-
Tolliver feud, sometimes as the Tolliver-Martin-Logan
vendetta. That is to say, the pleas of the residents not to
do away with their county after its period of almost
complete lawlessness were no doubt reinforced by the
awareness on the part of the Democratic majority in the
General Assembly that neighboring Fleming County
might go Republican, if the Republican portion of
Rowan were returned to it.

In any event, the particular history of Rowan
County, including the efforts of families to decimate
each other, has to be seen within the context of the
factionalism, chicanery, and struggles for dominance
that mark Kentucky's political history. That larger history provides a casebook on what can happen in a democratic land if its central government delegates the
major authority to its smaller political units and, still in
the spirit of laissez-faire, lets them proliferate at will,
while neglecting to establish a clear leadership post
within any of them. Individuals or groups fought for
power within the counties, while the counties struggled
against each other. According to Ireland, the rivalries
among Kentucky counties during the period of frenzied
railroad construction beginning in the 1860s was "not
unlike that between city-states of fourteenth century

Italy." Certainly he provides enough evidence to demonstrate the degree to which the individual counties were very nearly autonomous units, with the General Assembly serving primarily to rubber-stamp the bills coming to it from those with power or privilege in the "little kingdoms." For example, 1,034 of the 1,119 statutes passed by the assembly in 1873 were such bills; fearing "the wrath of special interests if they did not attend to their needs, the General Assembly inevitably put off to the end of the sessions proposals dealing with the Commonwealth's general needs." Hambleton Tapp and James C. Klotter, the authors of *Kentucky: Decades of Discord, 1865–1900,* describe the conditions under which the assembly met those "general needs" on the final night of the 1877–78 legislative term. To permit the passage of hundreds of bills, the house and senate set back their official clocks. A reporter who was present at the house session wrote that "as the apparently interminable conflict continued, the gentle flow of drinks increased, until at least one member was scuttled, and others though not overflowing were full." It was to celebrate the passage of the final bill, not a departing year (for the month was April), that those members who were still able to carry a tune sang "Auld Lang Syne."

If alcohol influenced the quality of the general laws passed by the General Assembly, it also played a dominant part in the county electoral process; saloons remained open during voting hours, and candidates bought votes with whiskey as well as with cash. In Rowan County, as elsewhere, voting was not by secret ballot but by voice, with the sheriff and other officials (as well as interested citizens, such as candidates running for their posts) present to keep a tabulation on how each person voted—and, of course, to be sure that those who had been bribed voted as they had promised to. The minority party in one county achieved a record vote in 1886 by renting a saloon and giving away free drinks. A newspaper in a southeastern Kentucky county reported that candidates "were trying, most laboriously, to float into office by way of groceries," "groceries" in those days serving as a synonym both for alcohol and the saloons that supplied it. Ireland recounts that a newly arrived citizen to Kentucky, one who had settled in "turbulent" Morehead, discovered, for the first time in his life, that candidates could buy votes. A smart voter would hold off until the election was about to close, for then he could get as much as fifty dollars from a candidate in a tightly contested race.

The Rowan County War ("in many ways," Ireland says with scholarly calm, "the most spectacular feud of nineteenth-century Kentucky") began within such an election-day environment, as the ballad inspired by its opening events shows. Though the following version, titled "The Tolliver Song," gets some of the names wrong, it is the one, codified by folk-song specialists, that Josiah H. Combs includes in his collection, *Folk-Songs of the Southern United States:*

It was in the month of August, all on election day,
Lent Martin, he was wounded, some say by Johnny Day.
But Martin could not believe it, or could not think it so;
He thought it was Bud Tolliver that struck the fatal blow.

They wounded young Ad Simon, although his life was
  saved;
He seems to shun grog shops since he stood near the grave.
They shot and killed Sol Bradley, a sober, innocent man;
Left his wife and children to do the best they can.

Martin did recover, some months had come and past;
All in the town of Morehead these men did meet at last.
Tolliver and a friend or two about the street did walk;
They seemed to be uneasy, with no one wished to talk.

They walked into Judge Carey's grocery, and stepped up to
  the bar;
But little did he think, dear friends, he had met his fatal
  hour.
The sting of death was near him; Martin rushed in at the
  door.
A few words passed between them concerning a row before.

People soon got frightened, began to rush out of the room,
When a ball from Martin's pistol laid Tolliver in the tomb.
His friends then gathered round him, his wife to weep and
  wail;
And Martin was arrested and placed in the county jail.

He was put in jail at Roand, there to remain a while,
In the hands of law and justice, to bravely stand his trial.
The people talked of lynching him, at present though they
    failed;
The prisoner's friends removed him to Winchester jail.

Some persons forged an order, their names I do not know;
The plan was soon agreed upon, for Martin they did go.
Martin seemed to be discouraged, he seemed to be in dread.
"They have sought a plan to kill me," to the jailer Martin
    said.

They put the handcuffs on him, his heart was in distress.
They hurried to the station, got on the night express.
Along the line she lumbered, just at her usual speed.
There were only two in numbers to commit the awful deed.

Martin was in the smoking car, accompanied by his wife.
They did not want her present when they took her husband's
    life.
And when they arrived at Farmer, they had no time to lose.
A band approached the engineer and bade him not to move.

They stepped up to the prisoner with pistols in their hands;
In death he soon was sinking, he died in iron bands.
His wife overheard the noise, being in the smoking car.
She cried, "O Lord! they've killed my husband," when she
    heard the pistols fire.

The death of these two men has caused trouble in our land,
Caused men to leave their families and take the parting band.
It has caused continual war, which may never, never cease.
I would to God that I could see our land once more in peace.

They killed our deputy sheriff, Baumgartner was his name.
They shot him from the bushes, after taking deliberate aim.
The death of him was dreadful, it may never be forgot;
His body was pierced and torn with thirty-two buckshot.

I composed this song as a warning. Oh, beware young men!
Your pistols will cause you trouble, on this you may
    depend.
In the bottom of a whiskey glass a lurking devil dwells,
Burns the breath of those who drink it, and sends their souls
    to hell.

2

If, during the six years my family lived in Morehead, I
had attended to the blind ballad singer at the bus depot
as he sang a variation of this song, I would have under-
stood a historical reason for the proscription of the selling of alcohol in Rowan County. Actually, I first
listened to the words of "The Tolliver Song" at
Cornell, while I was being interviewed for my new job
by the folklorist in my prospective department, a
scholar with a far greater knowledge about the past of
eastern Kentucky than I possessed. Nor did I know that
earlier and more famous blind singers had performed in
Rowan County; they included Blind Bill Day (a family
name that probably gives him a connection not only
with the "Johnny Day" of "The Tolliver Song," but at
a farther remove, with Bob Day, the Oldsmobile dealer
I talked with on many Morehead evenings), who seems

a likely source of the initial version of the ballad. According to Charles K. Wolfe's *Kentucky Country,* an account of the state's folk and country music, Blind Bill Day began "composing topical broadside ballads on local events as early as 1884, and either composed or popularized well-known songs like 'The Rowan County Feud' [another title for the ballad], 'The Coal Creek Troubles,' and 'The Murder of J. B. Marcum.' " In 1926, Day was performing for handouts before the Rowan County courthouse; the court stenographer, who a few years earlier had been a script girl in Hollywood for Cecil B. DeMille's first and silent version of *The Ten Commandments,* heard him as he played and sang "The Lady Went A-Hunting," and saw him as having show-business potential.

As a result of this encounter, both the stenographer, Jean Thomas (who later organized the American Folk Song Festival at Ashland and wrote a series of popular books, including *The Traipsin' Woman),* and Blind Bill became famous. In his case, though, he became a public figure as Jilson Setters, a name Jean Thomas dreamed up for him, no doubt because she thought it had more local color. Dressed up in carefully selected homespun clothes, carrying, in addition to a new name, two suitable props, "a ladderback hickory chair and an egg basket," Blind Bill was taken to New York for theater performances and radio broadcasts. A recent cataract operation had restored his sight. One wonders what that formerly blind minstrel made of himself and the world he was exposed to; so fully was his identity changed that even the Rowan County *News,* in its 1956 county centennial issue, refers to him only as Jilson Setters. The article about him in that issue says that, prior to his discovery by the courthouse stenographer with show-business connections, "he could be seen nearly any time with his fiddle in an oilcloth poke trudging along the creek, up a hollow or wherever there was a gathering of any kind. . . . Miss Jean Thomas," it continues, "took him to New York where he played in the opera house and the music was said to be the most perfect that ever had been heard. Later she took him to England where he played for the King and Queen."

In one of the many closets of our upstate New York farmhouse, which are jammed with castoffs and mementos, my wife found for me the yellowed and brittle pages of that bulky centennial issue of the Rowan County *News* after our return from Morehead and the Yucatan. Whatever the editor, W. E. ("Snooks") Crutcher, now deceased, said about the extent of her work on that issue, Jean remembers that her main job had been to make articles out of material submitted by merchants about the history and prospects of their firms. Stories like the one about "Jilson Setters" are not given attribution, but appear to be transcriptions of accounts by elderly citizens—recollections drawn from their own experiences or handed down from one generation to the next.

The first settlers in the county, who arrived during

the final decades of the eighteenth century, were, according to the centennial issue, "Mrs. Abbie Oxley and Mr. Ben Evans," whose last names still serve as the names of the small creeks that bisect the present county seat. These two settlers divided much of the area that was to become Morehead between them, Abbie Oxley taking the western section and Ben Evans the eastern. (A descendant of Ben Evans continued to reside in the eastern portion of town in the late 1950s, not far from our house on Caudill Court.) I suppose that they came into ownership of the land through Revolutionary War land grants, for the article containing their names says that "the first people to settle in Morehead for the most part came from Virginia on military grants." Others who settled in the county originally had destinations farther west in mind, but elected to stay because of the plentiful wildlife in the surrounding forests, the availability of land, and the lack of an Indian presence. Still, since Morehead was a way station on the Midland Trail, the majority of its early buildings—inns and taverns— were built for transients. The paucity of permanent residents was such that Andrew Jackson White, born in 1835 on what has become known as the Andy White Branch of Christy Creek, is commemorated by the Rowan County *News* as one of the "county's first citizens."

Twenty-six years younger than a far more famous native Kentuckian, Andy White was much like Lincoln, at least so far as his desire for education was concerned, and maybe the teller of the tale that is transcribed in the newspaper had Lincoln in mind. In Andy's youth, "schoolhouses were few and far apart. . . . Young Andy being determined to have an education would go on the high hills and gather a load of pine knots, then while the rest of the family would be sleeping at night young Andy would light a pine torch and stick it up in the corner of the fireplace . . . to make a light for him to study by and he would often study until after midnight."

The tale interests me both for what it includes and what it ignores. Andy White became "a school teacher, one among the best in those days. He taught school for 35 years and he was also a music teacher and taught music for 22 years." During the Civil War, a period in which Kentucky was officially neutral, its young men serving either for the Union or the Confederacy, Andy joined the rebel cause. Later, "he served as deputy sheriff under Squire Hogge. At the age of 55, he decided he would marry and settle down," and so "he won the heart" of Nancy Carter, a young widow, and the pair had seven children.

"In the latter years of his life," the storyteller continues, "he was not able to work much and he did a lot of reading, his favorite book being the Bible. He almost knew it by memory. The ministers of our vicinity would sometimes ask him where to find certain scriptures. He could tell them immediately what book of the Bible to look in and usually what verse of that book it was in. He had many friends and he sure enjoyed having them come and visit him which they would do quite often. He always had plenty of good country food on his table and no one ever left his home hungry close to meal time." He lived his entire eighty-six years on Andy White Branch at the headwaters of Christy Creek, dying there in February 1921.

What the storyteller neglects to mention is that Andy White's service as deputy sheriff under Squire Hogg (though his descendants spell the name with a final "e," he apparently didn't) coincided with the climactic months of the Rowan County War. During these months of heightened violence, White openly spoke of the Tolliver faction as "our side." The death, in 1885, of a previous deputy sheriff, Stewart Baumgartner (it is the "dreadful" ambush referred to in the penultimate stanza of "The Tolliver Song") took place at the head-waters of Christy Creek, close to Andy White's home. Baumgartner was a Republican and a supporter of the opposing Martin faction; he had a reputation for brutality. The ambush perhaps was a retaliation for the wounding, in the same general vicinity, of Z. T. (for Zachary Taylor) Young. Whatever his claims to objectivity, Young, the Democratic county attorney, lent the powers of his office to the Tolliver cause. Only circumstantial evidence—motive and a likely propinquity—connects Andy White to Baumgartner's death, and I may be the first, at least in recent years, to wonder about the possibility of his involvement. (There is no doubt about his involvement as a Tolliver partisan in a later event, one I have yet to relate.)

One can perhaps explain the seeming contradictions in such a figure as Andy White, by seeing him as a hospitable family man and self-educated teacher who, caught up in a second, if miniaturized, civil war (and one that more accurately can be termed a civil war than the attempt by the South to secede from the Union), elects through belief or necessity one side over another, and considers himself deputized and always on patrol to defeat the enemy. Given the political climate in much of the state, particularly in its eastern counties, any official —sheriff or his deputy, judge or justice of the peace or town marshal—must have felt himself far more responsible to his allies than to the general citizenry, or to the ineffectual government in Frankfort.

Indeed, the lawlessness to which White was such a willing contributor seems a continuation of Civil War conditions in the region that became Rowan County less than a decade before the cessation of those larger hostilities. "The Civil War," one article in the centennial issue recounts, ". . . was an age of guerrillas" in Morehead and the surrounding area. "These bands of men, mostly leaning toward the South, kept the villages in constant terror with their invasions and threatened raids. One of the worst raids came on Nov. 10, 1863, at Morehead, where the guerrillas entered the town early in the morning and held sway some time until they were finally driven off but without loss. Again on the

21st of March in 1864 the guerrillas entered Morehead and succeeded in destroying the courthouse by fire." Such guerrilla bands were interested less in supporting the Southern cause than in looting houses whose male occupants had left to become soldiers, whichever side they chose. According to another article, "The situation became so bad that a Captain Barbour of Morehead organized a society known as 'Home Guards' whose purpose it was to protect the women folk of the county" as well as to prevent theft; like similar self-appointed groups elsewhere, Barbour's men became known as "Regulators," and they "took the place of the official law forces of the county for some years."

Several state historians find that the history of terrorism and vigilantism in eastern Kentucky predates even the Civil War. Such was the case, of course, in the American West; for that matter, lawlessness and self-appointed posses seem typical of any frontier society. History, that sad chronicle of human disorder, is the account of societies moving toward or away from those periods of relative integrity, justice, and general enlightenment that now provide us with whatever hope or meaning our species has.

3

Since it lacks abundant supplies of coal, Rowan County was spared the ravaging of hills, streams, and people that came to other parts of Appalachia. It possesses clay of the sort that makes good bricks, including fire bricks, and so clay mines and refractories came to the county; since its land also holds a particular kind of bluish sandstone, known as Rowan County freestone because it splits easily in any direction, a number of quarries have been excavated. Until the hills were denuded of their virgin forests, timber—oak, pine, walnut, hemlock, and ash—was the major resource. Sawmills once proliferated, the largest apparently being the one described in the historical edition of the newspaper as "a million dollar sawmill at Rodburn" (a hamlet near Morehead, now celebrated only for its picnic grove) built by "the old Ixon-Rodburn Company from New York."

If timber brought the first railroad to Morehead (apparently one constructed by the Ixon-Rodburn Company or its successor), the development of the larger railroad system that became known as the Chesapeake and Ohio in turn intensified both logging and the manufacture of wood products, such as broom handles, wagon spokes, barrelheads, and railroad ties. In 1881, the first train to travel on the system's tracks arrived at Morehead; the centennial issue reports that "people came miles" to see it.

One might assume that the arrival of trains, the passenger cars lighted with kerosene lamps and heated with potbellied stoves, would, by lessening the county's insularity, diminish rather than exacerbate family rivalries. In the view of Stuart Sprague, a present-day historian at Morehead State University, however, the coming of the railroad brought enough new people into the area to create a political instability in a county that had typically given the Democratic party a narrow majority. In the August 1884 election for county sheriff, the Republican Cook Humphrey defeated the Democrat Sam Gooden by twelve votes.

The election-day violence that began the Rowan County War apparently started as a fist fight in a saloon. In the melee, John Martin, a Republican and a personal friend of Cook Humphrey, lost a tooth (as well as suffering other facial damage) to a "heavy instrument" apparently wielded, or so "The Tolliver Song" says, either by one of the Tollivers or John Day—the latter a deputy sheriff on the outgoing force. Allegedly, Martin drew a pistol. In the gun fight that followed, Solomon Bradley was killed—perhaps as he was rushing to the assistance of Adam Sizemore, who had been struck down by a bullet in his neck. No reliable evidence exists as to the person or persons responsible for the death and the wounding; the participants themselves might have been too frenzied and drunk to know.

Martin, who was a friend of Bradley as well as of newly elected Sheriff Humphrey, obviously thought that he, at least, knew who had injured him: Floyd Tolliver. And so, as "The Tolliver Song" reports (although mistaking Floyd for his cousin Bud), Martin killed Floyd Tolliver not long afterward in another saloon. Members of the two families, both prominent in the county, spread contradictory reports as to which of the two men had wanted to avoid bloodshed, and which had pulled out his gun first. According to the Martin version of the story, as it was later reported in the Louisville *Courier-Journal,* the "mortally wounded" Floyd Tolliver, "raising himself in his dying agonies" after his friends had rushed into the saloon, "said to them, 'Boys, remember what you swore to do; you said you would kill him, and you must keep your word.' "

In any event, the feud was on. As the ballad recounts faithfully enough, John Martin was removed to the Winchester jail to prevent Tolliver supporters from breaking into the Morehead jail to lynch him. Subsequently, a number of men (not two, as in the ballad version, but more likely as many as five) of the Tolliver faction brought a forged order to the Winchester jailer to release Martin to their custody, and the jailer—James Eeton by one account—reluctantly did so, despite the desperate pleading of the prisoner. The differences between "The Tolliver Song" and what actually took place are perhaps slighter than the differences from truth found in most such ballads. According to the account in the *Courier-Journal,* "Martin's wife was in Winchester, and she started back to Morehead on the same train that had her husband, although she was unaware of the fact. . . . When [long after dark] they reached Farmers, a little town in Rowan County, a few miles west of Morehead, the train was boarded by a large body of masked men. Martin was sitting handcuffed on a seat of

48

coach 38, of the Chesapeake and Ohio railroad. The men drew their pistols and filled him with lead. Although shot many times, he did not die until the train reached Morehead, and his wife knew not that her husband was on the same train until she was called to see him die."

The leader of the masked men, and undoubtedly the strategist of the entire ruse, was Craig Tolliver, Floyd's brother. Henceforward, he would be the subject of stories and editorials throughout the nation. I find it difficult to see him as an Andy White, one with a contradictory mixture of qualities. He demonstrated a final, reckless courage. He was also a ruthless killer and a bully who terrorized a community to such an extent that more than half of its citizens fled. The railroad, whose coming, by disrupting a tenuous political stability, may have precipitated the violence, and which served as a conduit for guns and ammunition as well as the scene of a dramatic slaying, was also the background for the end of the hostilities, as far as they can be said to end with Craig Tolliver's death. He was fatally shot during his escape from a hotel. Running down a lane, Tolliver almost managed to reach the railroad tracks; his body fell near the switch.

4

The issue of the Louisville *Courier-Journal* from which I've been quoting is that of Thursday morning, June 23, 1887. The front page is almost wholly devoted to the exploits of the previous day in Morehead and the history of the events leading up to them. Under the drawing of a mountaineer holding a whiskey bottle in one hand and a pistol in the other, the account begins:

CRAIG TOLLIVER.

LEXINGTON, June 22.—[*Special.*]—The news from Rowan to-day is of the most exciting character, as it appears to be an indisputable fact that Craig Tolliver is killed and his gang dismembered forever. The news comes by a Lexington minister and others, who came through Morehead to-day on the solid train from Norfolk, Va. At about 9:30 o'clock this morning, when this train was within a few miles of Morehead, it was flagged by some citizens, and when it came to a stop they informed the conductor that

A BLOODY BATTLE

was going on in Morehead between a Sheriff's posse and the Tolliver gang, and that it would not be safe for the train to proceed until hostilities ceased. The passengers and trainmen were very much frightened, and at their solicitation the conductor ran the train on to Martin's switch, two miles and a half east of Morehead. There they remained until nearly 12 o'clock, when they were notified that the fighting was over and that the train might safely pass through Morehead. The train stopped at Morehead for some time, and there the passengers viewed the slain and learned the particulars of the battle . . .

This front page, with its many columns of small print, whatever its inaccuracies, has served as one of the primary sources for historians of the Rowan County War. Another source is a detailed report made by Captain Ernest MacPherson, commanding officer of the state troops brought to Morehead to keep the peace during and after the August court session, at which the alleged killers of Craig Tolliver were acquitted. (His report is an attempt to explain as best he can "the peculiar predicament of Rowan county [that] renders it one of the curiosities of the nineteenth century.")

The events leading up to the Morehead battle include so many atrocities that, as one early chronicler (with a love to embellish each death with imaginative adjectives) complains, "to detail . . . [them] would prove tedious." One of the more important of these events was an attack led by Craig Tolliver, who had become town marshal and the dominant power in the local government. Having learned that Sheriff Humphrey and another Martin supporter, Benjamin Raybourn, were spending the night at the home of John Martin's widow, Tolliver organized a posse that managed to burn down the house, kill Raybourn, and jail two Martin daughters for no cause other than their lineage. His most-desired victim, Humphrey, who had wounded him inside the house, escaped into the surrounding woods.

Soon afterward, Humphrey resigned as sheriff, perhaps finding too uncomfortable the post to which he had been elected by such a narrow margin amid so much hostility. As he surely must have expected, a Tolliver partisan was elected to replace him; that new sheriff, William Raney, promptly attempted to arrest him. In the ensuing gun battle, which took place mostly within Howard Logan's store, Logan put himself on Humphrey's side; though Raney made no arrest, one of his bullets killed Logan's son.

On two occasions previous to the ultimate establishment of peace by MacPherson's detachment, troops arrived, but their attempts to end violence and bring justice failed before the continuing hostility of the factions, the mass of contradictory testimony, and the blatant bias of juries and judges. Though there were numerous trials for murder and other violent acts, the only killer to serve a prison term had no connection with the rival factions. (Actually, no more than two dozen people were killed during the Rowan County War; the preponderance of wounded among the casualties must have been the result of indifferent marksmanship.) Toward the close of the second occupation by the troops, the prosecutor who had arrived with them, unable to gain convictions of either Humphrey or Tolliver, arranged for a truce by having both of them sign documents in which they swore to depart permanently from the county. Humphrey left for Missouri, and remained in exile; Tolliver not only returned to town after the court adjourned, but consolidated his power by becoming police judge in an election even more controlled than earlier ones. With Humphrey gone, the Martin faction had lost even its residual strength.

Tolliver operated from his headquarters in the American House, a hotel he apparently had confiscated, much as he had taken another hotel for the use of the confederate elected to his former post as town marshal. According to *Kentucky: Decades of Discord, 1865–1890,* Tolliver, from his hotel, "took control of the whiskey business, which he operated without license," while (as another historian suggests) making himself a role model for all those aspiring to crime and violence. Though Charles G. Mutzenberg's *Kentucky's Famous Feuds and Tragedies* (1917) seems an attempt by a popularizer to take advantage of the nation's continuing fascination with bloodshed in Appalachia, it probably can be trusted even in its more lurid passages recounting Craig Tolliver's reign of terror. "Magistrates refused to issue warrants," Mutzenberg reports, "knowing that such an act would forfeit their lives. Had the warrants been issued, no officers could have been persuaded to execute them. The residences and grog shops of the Tollivers resembled and were arsenals. An effective and favorite method of Craig Tolliver to rid himself of any, to him, undesirable citizens, was to send a written communication to them, setting forth the fact that Rowan County could dispense with their presence, and that on a certain day in the near future certain funerals would take place unless they were gone from the county."

The new police judge also could obtain from willing county officials indictments of anybody whose actions or words displeased him. During the two years of his increasingly absolute rule, the population of the town diminished, according to one estimate, from seven hundred to fewer than three hundred citizens. Howard Logan was among the merchants and members of the professional class—the lawyers and doctors—who emigrated. A relative, Dr. Henry Logan, had also aroused Tolliver's displeasure. In what most commentators perceive as a bogus charge, Z. T. Young, who had relinquished to his son the position of county attorney, was able to secure Dr. Logan's indictment for conspiring to kill the county judge, as well as Young himself. While that physician, like John Martin before him, was waiting for his trial in the Winchester jail, Craig Tolliver led a posse that included Sheriff Hogg to his house a few miles out of town, ostensibly to arrest Logan's two sons on a warrant as false as the one that had imprisoned their father. Sprague, the Morehead State University historian, thinks that Tolliver might have wanted them out of the way, to prevent them from testifying at their father's upcoming trial. I suspect that Tolliver's love of power had become so obsessive that he needed no clear motive to sustain it by injuring or killing helpless people. With Tolliver's permission,

Hogg put out a fire the posse had lit on the Logan porch. Then, having coaxed the brothers—the younger eighteen, the older twenty-five but a consumptive weighing no more than a hundred pounds—from the house by promising them protection, Hogg fled from the scene as Tolliver and the others (according to Captain MacPherson's report) "opened fire and killed one of the boys, and then the other. The posse comitatus, or some of them, continued to fire shots into the dying or dead boys, and then left them where they fell." Hogg rejoined the posse for its return to Morehead. "On the brow of the hill overlooking the town," MacPherson continues, the posse halted, to be "instructed by Judge Tolliver that all should tell the same story: that is, that the Logan boys were killed in resisting a proper arrest, and only as an absolute necessity."

MacPherson says that Hogg "kept his knowledge of the affair a profound secret" as long as he could, though the truth obviously came out during the August court trials that MacPherson attended. If, as I assume, Hogg maintained his silence until the trials, he may have done so as much out of personal shame as fear for his own well-being. According to an article about Tolliver that appeared in the Lexington *Morning Transcript* two days after his death, he "had a good face; it was not brutal. His manners were mild so long as he was not aroused." That "good face," as well as his perversions, makes him the stuff of nightmares. Still, it is Hogg—the sheriff with no propensity for sadism, whose pity, maybe, forced him to run away from the very act he helped through cowardice to engender—who carries for me the greater threat, as representative of the part in all of us that makes such evil possible.

5

For this selective account of what Editor Crutcher called "the story of all the gruesome and seemingly inhuman killings and deeds of the Rowan County War" and refused to chronicle, I have largely depended upon the documents provided me by Jack D. Ellis, a former director of the Morehead State University library. Included, perhaps inadvertently, among the papers Ellis sent is a copy of a decade-old letter he wrote to somebody who had contacted him for information in connection with a proposed film on that war. If only a little alteration could turn the opening events into a folk song, the concluding events certainly lend themselves, without the slightest change, for use in a motion picture. Indeed, perhaps the project never came to fruition because the great Morehead battle, while a true story, has since become a convention in Western films, with an oppressed hero (entering the struggle at a late moment, he is the single major figure yet to be defined in my reconstruction of the events) taking matters into his own hands, and the villain dying with his boots either on or off. (Some accounts say that Tolliver swore to die with them on, and did. A more interesting report is that, having heard a prophecy that he would die with his boots on, he discarded them in the unsuccessful attempt to thwart his fate, and so ran barefooted to his doom.)

D. B. Logan (named like a number of other Rowan Countians for Daniel Boone), the twenty-eight-year-old lawyer most responsible for ending the tyranny, was a cousin of the murdered brothers; after their deaths, Tolliver, as he had done with so many others, banished Logan from town. The Commonwealth's adjutant general, Sam E. Hill, made a brief visit to Morehead in November 1887 and sent a report of his investigations to Governor S. B. Buckner (named not for a Kentuckian but for the South American patriot and idealist Simón Bolívar, whose final, disillusioned words about his attempt to unite the warring factions and nations of his hemisphere were the famous "We have ploughed the sea"). Among other references to Logan and Tolliver, Hill paraphrases a communication sent by the latter to the exile in which "Tolliver goaded him . . . [by saying] that he intended to rent out his house, and hire out his wife to make a living for herself and children, two in number."

No doubt the governor, still new to his post, already had heard of these matters from his predecessor, James Proctor Knott, whom Boone Logan had visited in

Frankfort in order to plead either for a return of the troops (a request denied because of the cost and the uselessness of such troops in the past) or for the loan of rifles from the state armory (a request likewise rejected, as being an illegal use of the Commonwealth's weaponry). According to *Kentucky: Decades of Discord, 1865–1900*, "the quiet-mannered Logan," realizing that "Knott was deeply sympathetic," then said to him (in a speech I've found quoted in other histories even though its first printed source seems to be the sometimes inventive Mutzenberg), " 'Governor, I have but one home and but one hearth. From this I have been driven by these outlaws and their friends. They have foully murdered my kinsmen. I have not before engaged in any difficulties—but now I propose to take a hand and retake my fireside or die in the effort.' " Something of this sort, though expressed in plainer phrases, may indeed have been said, since Adjutant General Hill casually reports to Governor Buckner that Governor Knott "suggested that the good people of the community should take the matter in hand and themselves suppress the outlawry. Thus advised," Logan purchased the weapons himself, and formed his own posse, though a number of the "good people" he assembled came from other counties: he wanted a force sufficient to crush the Tollivers, and so enlisted the support of nearly a hundred men.

Logan obeyed all the legal technicalities, securing a warrant, issued by the magistrate "under protest," as

MacPherson puts it, for the arrest of Tolliver, on the charge of the murder of his two young cousins, and then making sure that the warrant reached Sheriff Hogg. "It was agreed," MacPherson says in his meticulous accounting of a battle that lasted for two hours of nearly continuous firing,

that 'Squire Hogg should go to town on the morning of the 22d of June, 1887, and demand the surrender of Judge Tolliver and the others charged with the murder. On the night previous Boone Logan and his friends surrounded Morehead. The "High Sheriff" failed to keep his appointment, and did not approach the place [Morehead] until after the fighting had begun, and remained outside until it was over. About 8:30 o'clock on the morning of the 22d of June one Bryant was sent to Pigman's store for information as to the movements of the Tollivers. Returning to his comrades, he was seen by Craig Tolliver, who, with Jay Tolliver, ran down Railroad street and fired on Bryant, but missed him, and he escaped into the woods. As the two Tollivers were coming back, Boone Logan commenced firing. He was at once deserted by the men with him, but continued firing, which was returned by the two Tollivers until their Winchester rifle and revolver were emptied. They then ran from below the depot to the American House, Craig Tolliver's hotel, and, getting ammunition, were joined by Bud, Andy, Cal, and Cate Tolliver, [Hiram] Cooper, and others, and all started on a run for the Central Hotel. Craig and Andy were the first to reach the Central Hotel, leaving the others, and going through the alleys. Bud Tolliver, Cooper, and the rest, under constant fire from the brush, went on by way of Railroad street. Halting at the drug store, they fired into the brush and wounded one Madden [a possible error, if not in identification then in aim, for the Madden most likely to be involved, Bunk, was Craig's chief crony and his replacement as town marshal]. Bud Tolliver was here shot in the thigh. Cal and Cate, who were mere boys, helped Bud up the lane and hid him in the weeds back of Mal. Johnson's store. They then joined the others, who were all now at the Central Hotel. Cooper went out in front of the hotel, on Main street, and fired on some of Logan's men; he was shot through the breast, and retreated into the hotel. He got into a wardrobe in a back room up-stairs, and in this place of fancied security was again hit by a bullet fired from the front of the house.

The Central Hotel was surrounded, a cessation of fire ordered, and Boone Logan called to the Tollivers "to come out and they should not be hurt." A message of the same purport was delivered by a woman. She returned with Cate Tolliver, a boy of fifteen years of age, who was disarmed and unmolested. The others refusing to surrender, Logan, profiting by the tactics employed against his cousins, ordered his men to fire the building. The Tollivers at once broke from the place and started for the brush. Jay came out the rear way, got about fifty feet, was shot three times and fell. Craig and Andy came out the south side, and amid "a perfect hurricane" of bullets, Andy, with two small flesh wounds, succeeded in reaching the woods. Craig Tolliver's good luck at last deserted him. He started running, and firing as he ran, down the lane which leads from the Central Hotel to the 'railroad track. At the corner, and by the drug store, [Hiram] Pigman and [Ap] Perry and three others were posted. They opened fire on Tolliver, and the scores of others stationed about the Central Hotel continued their fire. Craig Tolliver went a few feet beyond the corner, fell, rose twice and fell again at the switch, literally riddled with rifle-balls and buck-shot.

═══

Though later he was to deny composing the message, newspapers throughout the nation reported that Boone Logan, upon winning the battle, telegraphed to the governor the four words, "I have done it." An approving article in the *New York World* said the telegram "excels somewhat the laconic bulletin of the great Caesar." A passenger on the train held up at Martin's switch for the duration of the battle was disappointed by Tolliver's death, for according to the *Courier-Journal* of June 23, he had "determined, if the train stopped long enough, to get off and try to see Craig Tolliver, of whom I had heard so much."

Despite Tolliver's death and the defeat of his forces, the remaining members of his faction—and here Andy White's complicity with them becomes most evident—wanted the war to continue. After the acquittal of Pigman and Perry, the two men accused of Tolliver's murder, Captain MacPherson observed what seemed to him a conspiratorial conversation among White and other Tolliver supporters. MacPherson found in a railroad car a shipment of rifles consigned to Deputy Sheriff White; this aborted attempt to renew the conflict and take revenge for Tolliver's death was possibly funded by Z. T. Young.

Aftershocks reverberated for years beyond that, of course. Dr. Louise, who is related to the Tollivers through her mother, told Jean and me that one of her earliest memories, from her fourth year, is of standing with a sister at a courthouse window during a visit with their father, a circuit court judge, and seeing a great-uncle shot down and killed on the courthouse lawn by Martin men. It was the last murder to be directly attributed to the feud. "I expect he had been drawn there by a ruse," Louise said. He was Cate Tolliver, who, as a fifteen-year-old, had survived the great Morehead battle by surrendering outside the Central Hotel.

THE PAST:
A CRUSADE

1

The issue of the Rowan County *News* celebrating the county's centennial devotes a section to the history of the college. "The year 1887," the opening of a long story on the origins of that institution says,

> was a memorable one for Morehead and Rowan County, for it marks the end of the county's most crucial period and the beginning of its regeneration.
>
> Reverberations of the devastating Rowan County War were still echoing in these hills when a young minister and his mother, Frank and Phoebe Button, came as strangers to Morehead and laid the foundations of the Morehead Normal School.

Indeed, it was the notoriety given to the town by Craig Tolliver, as well as the opportunity provided by his death, that attracted the pair to town shortly after the great battle of Morehead. The article quotes part of a speech made by J. Harlan Powers, a local attorney who had been one of the school's first pupils, at the 1954 dedication of Morehead State College's auditorium to the memory of Frank Button. "These devoted people," Powers declared, "being inspired with the missionary spirit, and believing that the salvation of this section was in the teaching of the Bible and in

Christian education of the children . . . turned to Morehead as a field for their labor."

The Buttons arrived in Morehead without resources to build or staff much of a school; initially, it was situated in their home and opened in the fall of 1887 with one student for the son and his mother to teach. Frank Button, who had just been graduated from the Lexington College of the Bible, secured a small livelihood by assuming the pastorship of the local Christian church, the one in which Dr. Louise was later to be baptized, and of which she remains a member. That church, like all the others in Morehead, had suffered during the years of violence and despotism. Its services were so intermittent and poorly attended that, according to a biographical account of the Buttons in the centennial issue, "it had practically ceased to function."

The State Board of the Christian Church contributed a small sum to the new school, including a $500 donation given for that purpose by William Temple Withers, a Lexington resident and former Confederate general, who over the years made further financial gifts to a cause he believed in—a school to prepare teachers who would spread Christian morality and general knowledge throughout its region. A former Morehead resident donated land for the campus, and relatives of the Buttons from their Illinois hometown gave $1,500 for the construction of a boarding hall. Until 1900, the operating expenses of both the local church and the new school were mainly provided by the Kentucky Christian Missionary Society; in 1900, the normal school came under the jurisdiction of a national organization of the same church, the Christian Women's Board of Missions.

That board brought almost immediate improvements to the school. It gave funds to enlarge the facilities, teaching staff, course offerings, and student body. The school, now fully accredited, offered a four-year high school curriculum and provided scholarships for mountain students it found deserving. Some of these were working scholarships in a newly established printing plant and broom factory. Departments were established in biblical study, music, and teaching; students could elect to follow a college preparatory program, or one that prepared them for teaching.

Ida Button, Frank's daughter, was another speaker at the dedication of Button Auditorium, and the centennial issue includes her reminiscences about the early decades of the school. "I can see students arriving on horseback or in wagons, with no advance registration, no money for tuition, but they had faith that here they could find an education for which they yearned," she recalled. "I remember hearing my father talk about them and my mother asking, 'What did you do?' and his reply, 'They have come so far, I can't send them home.' No one ever knew where all the scholarships came from."

Ida was born of the 1889 marriage of Frank to Hattie

Bishop, a Morehead native, but from the sparsity of references to Hattie in the centennial issue, I assume that she had little to do with the school so central to the lives of her husband and mother-in-law. Frank and Phoebe's attachment to each other seems to me a central fact in their lives, the depth of it perhaps related to two deaths, father and husband, sister and daughter, that left them the only survivors of their family. To support herself and her remaining child, Phoebe taught school in her native town of Oquawka, Illinois. When Frank was about twelve, the pair departed for Midway, Kentucky, where the mother had been offered a teaching job at the Female Orphan's School. The centennial issue reports that Frank "achieved the distinction of becoming its only boy graduate." Phoebe was forty-seven and Frank twenty-one when they arrived in Morehead to ameliorate through Christian education the conditions that had brought so much violence to the region.

According to a newspaper article my wife wrote in 1951 that contrasted the inauguration of a new president of the college with the arrival of the first head of the Normal School in 1877 (derived from the French *école normale,* that title once was commonly employed for a school that trained teachers), "His first day in town, Dr. Button was forced to duck behind an old stone chimney to avoid getting hit by an exchange of bullets in the city street." An extant letter from General Withers to Frank Button, telling him that the animosity directed against his new school would give it needed publicity, suggests that some residents wanted no strangers bent on moral uplift to interfere with their lives, however endangered they themselves might be by random lead pellets.

Whether helped or hindered by antagonism to them, Phoebe and Frank persevered, nurturing their venture so successfully that by 1904 their school had trained three hundred teachers. In addition to his duties as administrator, teacher, and pastor, Frank became a kind of nurse to the growing student flock, attending to the needs, for example, of a whole dormitory of boys afflicted with measles; and he also served for a time as mayor of Morehead. Phoebe seems to have given herself more fully to teaching than did her son, though the author of a Christian Women's Board of Missions report, referring to her as "one of the best women I have ever known," praises her "movements among the people," the "kind words and deeds" which made her "known and loved by all the community." Described as a frail woman even at the time of her arrival in Morehead, she died in 1892 "following a serious illness which many felt was occasioned by her heavy work and responsibilities."

Her son must have agreed with that assessment of the cause of her physical decline; devoted as he was to the school, he abdicated his position in a fruitless attempt to help her regain her health in a less demanding environment elsewhere in the state. After her death, he responded to a call to return as the school head, but left once again in 1911 to become State Supervisor of Rural Schools, a position funded by the Rockefeller Foundation. Perhaps the death of his mother contributed to the apparent ebbing of his commitment to the school which he, with her help, had founded. He did return once again, though, as first president, when the normal school was merged into the state system in 1923 as the Morehead State Normal School—a political coup for his hometown managed by Z. T. Young's son Allie, now a state senator. During Button's tenure as president, the school added "and Teachers College" to its name, having been given the right in 1927 to award college undergraduate degrees. In 1930, the year of his retirement, the school became simply Morehead State Teachers College.

"Doctor" or "Brother" Button—throughout his years in Morehead he was called by one or the other of these titles—died in 1933. Whatever his piety, he had not become a zealot, or one who aspires through oratory to raise the religious enthusiasm of the masses. In a tribute read at the 1954 ceremony that gave his name to the college auditorium, he was called "quiet and unassuming," a man who "plodded slowly along, never letting up until his goal was accomplished," words that make him seem dull but steady. Whatever his temperament, he had already been relegated to an earlier epoch, for he was seen in the same tribute as "a man representing the missionary spirit of years past. . . ."

Only two years before my appointment to the school

Button had founded, its name was further shortened to
Morehead State College, a title that took away completely its original emphasis as a normal school to edu-
cate young people so that through their own classrooms
they could impart Christian learning to a violent and
godless world. But now—nearly forty years after my
appointment—I realize that a form of the missionary
spirit still existed there in 1950 and that I had been very
much a willing part of it, for the Christian message had
been transformed or mitigated into a humanistic one. I
was one of four new members appointed into a veteran
department. According to the white-haired and kindly
president who had interviewed me, the infusion of so
many newcomers into one department, an unusual
increase for such a small college, was the consequence
of his desire to bring humanistic culture and general
enlightenment to a portion of the country that geography had isolated. Assuming our rightness and intellec-
tual superiority, we rudely displaced the courses,
methods, and pieties of the two teachers from an earlier
era still in the department, one a former clergyman and
the other a survivor of the first staff to be appointed
when the state took over the school.

As a veteran teacher at Cornell, I have become to
younger professors and entering doctoral candidates as
much an anachronism, I suppose, as I found those two
elderly Morehead colleagues to be. Maybe we must be
displaced ourselves before we can look with any kind of
comprehension or empathy at a previous order that we

had helped to displace. Stuart Sprague, the historian at Morehead State University who has written extensively on the region, remarks that a belief in Christian education was "commonplace among those who attributed the feuds to ignorance and lack of religion," and "gave rise to an 'uplift movement,' creating a number of 'academies' in feud-ridden counties." His words are professionally objective; they neither affirm nor deny that an institution like the Morehead Normal School made a difference. But if change is an inevitable process, one can say at least that people like D. B. Logan, who ended a tyranny, and Frank and Phoebe Button, who commenced a school, were agents of that process in Morehead.

I suppose the success of Morehead Normal School is to be gauged by the graduates with teaching certificates it sent into the countryside, the idealistic young teachers who actually took ill-paying jobs in decrepit, one-room schoolhouses. Two graduates became well known for their work in education. Harlan Hatcher, a 1919 graduate, became a respected scholar and administrator who was appointed president of the University of Michigan, thus inaugurating a lengthy series of highly competent local graduates who left the area for greater opportunities elsewhere. His achievements were remarkable, but those of Cora Wilson Stewart were extraordinary. Despite a growing national and even international reputation in education, she never renounced her allegiance to her native region. She enrolled in the Morehead Normal School in 1890, when she was fifteen, gaining her teaching certificate two years later; she developed a lasting friendship with Frank Button and served as a member of the school's advisory board.

Cora Wilson Stewart's mission was that of a crusader against illiteracy, and its religious nature was never lost on her. The public speeches she made that remain in print all carry the repetitions and rhythms of an evangelist. "Those who delight in transferring to canvas the beauties of earth and sky," she said in the concluding paragraph of a major address on "The Elimination of Illiteracy" at the 1918 convention of the National Education Association,

> in tracing fair form and beauteous color may do it; those who delight in transforming marble block into figures of noble proportion and speaking likeness may do it; those who delight in perfecting the form and fragrance and color of flowers and in enriching the flavor and hue of fruits may do it; those who delight in impressing first lessons upon the plastic mind of a little child, molding his character and coloring his very soul, may do it; but let it be mine to carry the light to the illiterate man as he sits in his mental darkness, straining his eyes gazing after his vanished opportunity, and agonizing in his secret soul over the precious thing which he has lost. Let it be mine to bring to him a new opportunity, a new hope, and a new birth. It is a task too holy, too Christ-like for me, I must confess, but I crave that merit and that alone which will fit me for this task.

The zeal of this Morehead Normal School graduate obviously exceeded that of her mentor there. Her speech at the convention was so persuasive that the N.E.A. called for national support of her efforts in Kentucky and put Mrs. Stewart in charge of a newly created illiteracy committee of its own. But her most extraordinary accomplishment came early in her career, and it connects her, through a mutual concern for the welfare of the most neglected citizens of their region, with the future Dr. Louise. That practitioner was a nine-year-old child when Cora Stewart undertook to wipe out illiteracy within the adult population of largely rural Rowan County.

2

Cora Wilson Stewart was born in 1875 on a farm in Powell County about fifty miles southwest of Morehead. Her father, Jeremiah Wilson, was a physician who did some early school teaching to support his medical studies; he married a fellow Powell County teacher, Anne Halley, and the pair had seven children. Cora was the third to be born, but the first to survive early childhood.

In 1880, the family moved to Cross Roads, a village in Rowan County. In this community, Cora's father began his medical practice and, with her mother, operated a general store. Soon after their arrival, the village was renamed Farmers—the stop on the railroad where, one December night in 1884, Craig Tolliver and others boarded a train during its scheduled stop to kill the manacled John Martin. Some of the participants in the developing feud lived nearby and no doubt shopped at the Wilsons' store; in any event, Cora as a child was acquainted with a number of them. Later, that vendetta became the subject of her first published article ("The Rowan County War," published in the August 1902 issue of *The World Wide Magazine),* and a handy reference for her of the need for education in the speeches she gave while campaigning against illiteracy.

Since her father was frequently away, his growing practice taking him into more distant areas, Cora developed the closer attachment with her mother. As the eldest child, she helped her mother care for her younger brothers and sisters and aided her in the cooking and washing.

The fullest account of her life is found in an admirable, but unpublished, University of Kentucky master's thesis, Willie Everette Nelms's 1973 *Cora Wilson Stewart: Crusader Against Illiteracy.* Nelms remarks that Cora's mother "sprinkled her daily conversation with quotations from the Bible and urged her children to follow the trainings of Christ." According to Nelms, Cora said in her later years that her mother was the greatest influence on her life. Emulating her mother's piety, Cora, in her ninth year, began "regular pilgrimages into the woods to pray, and she continued this practice until she reached maturity." (In a section devoted to that period of Cora Stewart's life in which she had become a speaker in demand throughout the country, both for her eloquence and her reputation as the major authority on illiteracy in the nation, Nelms says that she "would kneel and pray for guidance" before every address, and "began every day by reading the Bible." The optimism she felt toward her crusade against illiteracy "was based increasingly on the belief that she was in harmony with God." In a 1926 letter she wrote, "I believe that our Heavenly Father has called me to a mission. To speak and write and work in behalf of all illiterate men and women whose eyes are blind to His word and whose lives are limited and darkened by ignorance.")

When Cora was four, she declared that she (like her mother) was going to be a teacher; a year later, according to Mrs. Wilson, she "was conducting mock classes in the backyard and demanding that her students address her as 'Miss Cora.' "

She became an adept reader before beginning school in the one-room schoolhouse in Farmers, which (like the majority of its eastern Kentucky counterparts) had a dirt floor, no glass in its windows, and plank benches. Her parents had a collection of books and a neighboring family had more, and soon she had read everything in both libraries. The neighbors were the only people in the area to subscribe to a magazine, a fiction periodical called the *Old Arm Chair*. By the age of seven, Cora went to the neighbors' house regularly to read that magazine, the only new literature available to her; once, she "pulled down one of her father's medical volumes, almost as big as she was, and is said to have announced, 'If you don't get me something else to read, I'll have to read the doctor books.' "

The family moved to Morehead in 1890. It was the most convenient location for Dr. Wilson's practice, and there the precocious eldest child could attend the normal school. Cora, who was fifteen, not only enrolled in Morehead Normal but was hired as an assistant primary instructor in the public school. She continued her work in the public school after getting her teaching certificate; between sessions, she took further courses at National Normal University in Lebanon, Ohio.

Upon finishing her Lebanon studies in 1893, she left the public school to teach at Morehead Normal, and became active in church and civic work in town. A contemporary describes her at this period as less beautiful than "handsome"—a woman "five feet five inches tall" with "dark brown hair and eyes" who "enhanced her appearance with attractive clothes and careful grooming."

Restlessness marks her early professional life, as if she were searching for a cause as yet undefined, something larger than herself to which—like one of George Eliot's ardent and generous-spirited heroines—she could offer her intelligence and vitality. And so, after serving only two years on the Morehead Normal staff, she resigned, to teach in rural schools in the county. Boarding with various hill families, she discovered, Nelms says, "their desire for education. Her respect for their staunch character and native intelligence developed into a feeling of admiration which she retained for the rest of her life." (In reading her published writings, particularly her book entitled *Moonlight Schools,* which was published by E. P. Dutton in 1922, a reader today is apt to feel uncomfortable and perhaps even embarrassed by her praise of the mountaineers, emphasizing as it does their English, Scotch, Irish, and Welsh ancestry and distinguishing their "blood and bearing" from those of "inferior people" of "degenerate stock"—despite that present-day reader's realization that the author obviously was trying to counter the national prejudice toward mountain people as the inferior and degenerate ones.)

Whatever her admiration of rural people, two years of teaching their children in one-room schoolhouses was enough. Though it seems an erratic choice for one with her sensibility and aspirations, she elected to follow a business career, enrolling in the Commercial College of Kentucky University in Lexington in 1899. She did so well in that one-year program that she was asked to remain as a teacher, the first woman ever appointed to such a post at the college. (She was to become the "first woman" appointed to a number of subsequent positions.) Because of the illness of her mother, who was dying of tuberculosis, she taught at the school for less than a year. Upon the death of her mother, she became a secretary for a lumber company in Huntington, West Virginia, a job she apparently took in order to help her brothers and sisters complete their education. (Her father didn't die until 1917; I don't know the reason for this apparently skilled and busy physician's lack of adequate support of his children, or for his virtual disappearance, after moving his family to Morehead, from all biographical accounts of Cora Wilson Stewart's life, including Nelms's detailed thesis.)

Up to this point, her experiences resemble those of many talented women of her own and other epochs who struggle, without great success, to find a personal direction and goal other than the one provided by marriage, and whose family loyalties eventually entrap them. But in 1901, the Democratic party in Rowan County asked Cora to return from Huntington to run for the post of county school superintendent in the upcoming elections, a position that no woman had ever gained. She gave her energies, intelligence, and developing oratorical skill to that campaign, and won by a substantial margin over her male opponent.

3

Little public attention was paid to Cora Wilson Stewart during the years my family lived in Morehead. In researching some background information on the college for the issue of the school newspaper celebrating the inauguration in 1951 of a new president, Charles R. Spain, my wife discovered not only the detail about Frank Button finding refuge behind a chimney from the bullets spraying the streets on the day of his arrival, but an account of Cora Stewart's establishment of the Moonlight Schools. Surprised by the drama and success of Mrs. Stewart's endeavor, Jean wrote a story for the paper that, except for a later article in the issue of the Rowan County *News* celebrating the county's centennial, was the only reference, whether in conversation or in print, to that woman's accomplishments that I ever came across during the six years of our stay in town. Morehead, in those days, was not finding pride in its past, and it is likely that the campaign against illiteracy was associated too closely in the memory of its citizens with the ignorance and killing that had preceded it.

Attitudes of the townspeople toward their community and its history gradually changed in the years following our departure. A September 1961 issue of the Rowan County *News* carries an account of the closing of all Morehead businesses for the groundbreaking ceremonies presaging the construction of the St. Claire Medical Center. (A streamer above the headline declares, "Greatest Day Since College Established.") Adron Doran, the college president, gave the principal address; indeed, the future expansion of the college into a university depended upon the construction of a modern hospital. The growth of both institutions, accompanied by much publicity, of course had much to do with alterations in the community's sense of itself.

In 1973, Morehead State University brought to campus and there restored "Little Brushy School," the first one-room rural structure in which Cora Wilson Stewart taught. It serves as a museum of, and tribute to, her work. The university now has an Appalachian Adult Education Center and a Department of Adult and Continuing Education dedicated to furthering the service to adults that Mrs. Stewart began; the center's library has assembled materials by and about her that augment the Stewart collection in the University of Kentucky archives in Lexington.

It is surprising, in these days of resurgent feminism, that no researcher as yet has resurrected the struggles and triumphs of Cora Wilson Stewart. The best study of her life remains that unpublished master's thesis on a University of Kentucky library shelf. Active at a time in which women's rights were becoming a crucial part of the progressive movement, Cora Stewart supported women's suffrage and worked for the election of females to whatever offices they could then obtain. She was acquainted with some of the major suffragists, male as well as female, and got help for her nationwide campaign against adult illiteracy from Carrie Chapman Catt, the president of the National American Woman Suffrage Association; Jane Addams of the Hull House in Chicago; the Kansas journalist William Allen White, and many others. She herself was elected the first woman president of the Kentucky Educational Association. She was then elected to the executive committee of the National Education Association and in 1929 was appointed by President Hoover to chair the Executive Committee of the National Advisory Committee on Illiteracy, a body she was instrumental in creating. She also was instrumental in founding the illiteracy section of the World Conference on Education, and she presided over its sessions in Edinburgh, Geneva, Toronto, San Francisco, and Denver.

As a delegate to the national Democratic convention in San Francisco in June 1920, Mrs. Stewart gave the seconding speech for Ohio governor James M. Cox as that party's candidate for president, and became, following a vote for a prominent Kentucky suffragist, Laura M. Clay, on an earlier ballot, the second woman in American history to receive a vote for presidential nomination. In 1925, a popular magazine, the *Pictorial Review,* gave her a $5,000 achievement prize for her "contribution . . . to advance human welfare"— money she promptly used to further her work against illiteracy. In 1930, the National Council of Administrative Women gave her the Ella Flagg Young medal for distinguished educational service, an award that Mrs. Stewart, in accepting it in the name of all who were engaged in the national battle against illiteracy, construed "as a commission, as a mandate to carry on, for we have made only a beginning."

During her lifetime, she carried her crusade against

illiteracy across America, not only into the various states, but into prisons and Indian reservations, and into predominantly Negro communities as well as white ones; and during the First World War her methods and a text she had written for soldiers were used in army camps to teach conscripts how to read and write. She became so widely known that five of her speeches on the adult illiteracy movement were broadcast nationally by CBS radio, and another by NBC. Near the end of her life she was scheduled to appear as a subject of a weekly radio program, "This Is Your Life," but was too ill to attend.

Cora Stewart's later campaigns were modeled upon and given impetus by her initial one, made while she was serving her second term as school superintendent, to abolish illiteracy in Rowan County. Its remarkable record buoyed her despite considerable sufferings in her personal life and the inevitable setbacks to her national crusade. The attention paid by the *New York Times* and other metropolitan newspapers to the success of the Moonlight Schools in Rowan County gave her the reputation she needed to get legislative and financial support for her larger missions.

Once, following the defeat by the Kentucky legislature of a proposal of hers, Cora Stewart returned home to Morehead for a considerable stay. A questioner asked her if she had retired from her battles. Certainly it was that initial triumph in Rowan County that gave her the temerity to respond, "You must not get the impression that I have given up [the struggle against illiteracy]. I am only enlarging it. My aim of ten years service to my State, ten to my nation, and ten to the world is now entering the second chapter."

It was during this seeming hiatus at home that she began writing *Moonlight Schools,* that account of the educational experiment in Rowan County; it achieved its promotional purpose, which was to prepare the way for the second and third chapters.

4

As the new century was beginning, Cora Wilson apparently decided to embrace life as fully as she could; she attempted marriage as well as politics and public service. Little is known about her first marriage to Grant Carey, a Morehead youth (it goes unmentioned in Nelms's thesis) except that it lasted only a year. Several years later, in 1904, as she was nearing the end of her first term as county school superintendent, Cora was married again, this time to one of the teachers who served under her, Alexander T. Stewart. Though she was to be chosen once again to that office, she did not run in the 1905 race; Nelms conjectures that she "refused to stand for re-election" because of "the stress that her superintendent's duties placed on her husband," and adds that the death of the Stewarts' ten-month-old son in 1908 increased the tension between the couple.

No matter how generously made, a submission to the wishes of another can lead to mutual resentment, and possibly the voluntary relinquishing of her position helped to hasten rather than postpone the dissolution of the marriage. In any event, Mrs. Stewart found it impossible to remain at home, a dutiful wife. Asked to give speeches throughout the state, she accepted many offers and conducted a number of teacher institutes as well. Whatever these public activities, she must have felt dissatisfied and unfulfilled, and so in 1909 successfully campaigned to regain her office. Nelms, who examined the depositions and other legal papers filed in the University of Kentucky library relating to the divorce proceedings in 1910, finds evidence there that while "she performed the chores of the normal housewife . . . her husband was not happy with her conduct. He refused to work, became extremely jealous of his wife, and often stayed out late at night. Seeking escape from reality, he turned to drinking and became a domestic tyrant." She filed for divorce only after "her drunken husband returned home late one night, kicked open the door, and threatened to kill her. He searched out a pistol, took aim at her, and pulled the trigger. Luckily, the gun misfired, and Mrs. Stewart was able to get out of the house before he tried again."

Cora Stewart suffered what her friends considered "a profound melancholy" following the death of her child and the failure of her second marriage—and no doubt the vituperation against her character for being twice divorced contributed to that melancholy. In that era and place, one divorce was sufficient to bring censure, especially upon the woman. Apparently she gained a gradual release from her depression through ever-intensifying public service. As county superintendent, she started vocational classes for rural pupils in which, Nelms reports, "they cleared roadways and practiced building roads. [For years, the building or improvement of rural roads was to be one of her persistent, if secondary, causes.] Out of lumber cut from the surrounding woods, they made bookcases, picture frames, and furniture for the schools." She brought a horticulturist to the county, and, following his advice, encouraged the farmers in the area to plant fruit trees and such suitable, but ignored, crops as corn. Later, she organized fruit and corn clubs that held competitions to determine the growers with the largest harvests. Such achievements added to her statewide reputation as an administrator as well as a speaker. In 1911, the year of her election to the presidency of the Kentucky Education Association, she instituted the Moonlight School program for rural adults in Rowan County—the start of a project that gave purpose to the rest of her life and provided her with a kind of fulfillment never to be found in marriage.

5

In *Moonlight Schools,* and in many of her speeches and published articles, Cora Stewart refers to three people who provided her with the incentive to develop a program for others like them. Her anecdotes about the three become the parts of a single account, whose simple details are generalized into a call; it is a story that shows that Mrs. Stewart's persuasive skill as orator is matched by her controlled but still evangelical writing style.

"When I was Superintendent of Rowan County schools," Mrs. Stewart remarks in *Moonlight Schools* to open the story that became known to thousands of Americans of her day as an illustration of the nation's inner potential,

> I acted as voluntary secretary to several illiterate folk—a mistaken kindness—I ought to have been teaching them to read and write. Among these folk there was a mother whose children had all grown up without learning save one daughter who had secured a limited education, and when grown, had drifted away to the city of Chicago, where she profited by that one advantage which the city possessed over the rural district—the night school. She so improved her education and increased her efficiency that she was enabled to engage, profitably, in a small business. Her letters were the only joys that came into that mother's life and the drafts which they contained were the only means of relieving her needs. Usually she

would bring those letters to me, over the hill, seven miles, to read and answer for her. Sometimes she would take them to the neighbors to interpret. Once after an absence of six weeks, an unaccustomed period, she came in one morning fondling a letter. I noticed an unusual thing—the seal was broken.

Anticipating her mission, I inquired, "Have you a letter from your daughter? Shall I read and answer it for you?"

She straightened up with more dignity and more pride than I have ever seen an illiterate assume—with more dignity and more pride than an illiterate *could* assume as she replied, "No, I kin answer hit fer myself. I've larned to read and write!"

"Learned to read and write!" I exclaimed in amazement. "Who was your teacher, and how did you happen to learn?"

"Well, sometimes I jist couldn't git over here to see you," she explained, "an' the cricks would be up 'twixt me an' the neighbors, or the neighbors would be away from home an' I couldn't git a letter answered fer three or four days; an' anyway hit jist seemed like thar was a wall 'twixt Jane an' me all the time, an' I wanted to read with my own eyes what she had writ with her own hand. So, I went to the store an' bought me a speller, an' I sot up at night 'til midnight an' sometimes 'til daylight, an' I larned to read an' write."

To verify her statement, she slowly spelled out the words of that precious letter. Then she sat down, and under my direction, answered it—wrote her first letter— an achievement which pleased her immeasurably, and one that must have pleased the absent Jane still more.

A few days later a middle-aged man came into the office, a man stalwart, intelligent and prepossessing in appearance. While he waited for me to dispatch the business in hand, I handed him two books. He turned the leaves hurriedly, like a child handling its first books, turned them over and laid them down with a sigh. Knowing the scarcity of interesting books in his locality, I proffered him the loan of them. He shook his head.

"I can't read or write," he said. Then the tears came into the eyes of that stalwart man and he added in a tone of longing, "I would give twenty years of my life if I could."

A short time afterward, I was attending an entertainment in a rural district school. A lad of twenty was the star among the performers. He sang a beautiful ballad, partly borrowed from his English ancestors but mostly original, displaying his rare gift as a composer of song.

When he had finished, I went over and sat down beside him. "Dennis," I said, "that was a beautiful ballad. It is worthy of publication. Won't you write a copy for me?"

His countenance, which had lighted up at my approach, suddenly fell, and he answered in a crest-fallen tone, "I would if I could write, but I can't. Why, I've thought up a hundred of 'em that was better'n that, but I'd fergit 'em before anybody come along to set 'em down."

These were the three incidents that led directly to the establishment of the Moonlight Schools. I interpreted them to be not merely the call of three individuals, but the call of three different classes; the appeal of illiterate mothers, separated from their absent children farther than sea or land or any other condition than death had power to divide them; the call of middle-aged men, shut out from the world of books, and unable to read the Bible or the newspapers or to cast their votes in secrecy and security; the call of illiterate youths and maidens who possessed rare talents, which if developed might add treasures to the world of art, science, literature and invention.

The period was a magical one in the history of Rowan County, for not only were the rural people ready to learn, but the rural teachers, abetted by Cora Stewart's persuasive abilities, were so eager to help that at a staff meeting she had called to explain her plan "not one of them," she says, "expressed a doubt or offered an excuse, but each and every one of them . . . volunteered to teach at night, after she had taught all day, and to canvass her district in advance to inform the people of the purpose of these schools and to urge them all to attend."

Because of poor roads and the caution that had become a habit since the Rowan County War, the rural people, Mrs. Stewart says, "were not accustomed to venturing out much after night." So she scheduled the opening of classes for September 5, 1911, the night of the full moon. Although the nightly sessions afterward paid no attention to moon phases, lasting as they did Monday through Thursday for eight weeks, the phrase

"Moonlight Schools" attached itself to the educational movement, not only in Rowan County, but in many other regions, first in Kentucky and then elsewhere in the nation.

At that meeting of the teachers, the group had estimated an initial enrollment of 150 adults, three from each district. The teachers assembled at the fifty one-room schoolhouses. "We waited with anxious hearts," Mrs. Stewart says in her book, showing a talent for suspense.

> The teachers had volunteered, the schools had been opened, the people had been invited but would they come? They had all the excuses that any toil-worn people ever had. They had rugged roads to travel, streams without bridges to cross, high hills to climb, children to lead and babes to carry . . . ; but they were not seeking excuses, they were seeking knowledge, and so they came. They came singly or hurrying in groups, they came walking for miles . . . , they came bent with age and leaning on canes, they came twelve hundred strong!

6

Given the sparsity of the county's population, one would assume that the first year of the Moonlight Schools probably had exhausted the pool of interested adults; but when sessions were offered the following year, an even greater number—sixteen hundred this time—enrolled, many of them inspired by the new ability of neighbors to read and write.

Moonlight Schools is illustrated both with photographs and copies of letters written by students to Superintendent Stewart as demonstrations of their newfound literacy. Each who could write such a letter received a Bible, a gift valued not only for its contents by those who could now read it, but as a kind of commencement certificate. Graduates included a number of formerly illiterate preachers who had previously depended on sometimes barely literate members of their congregation to find scriptural passages that could serve as a basis for their sermons. Mrs. Stewart remarks that one preacher told his flock that "Peter was a fisherman and Paul was an oyster man," for his reader had turned "austere" into that word; another minister, having been read the sentence "Jacob made booths for his cattle," misconstrued it as "boots for his cattle," and so, Mrs. Stewart says, "discoursed from the pulpit on 'Jacob, that humane man [who] would not even permit his cattle to go barefooted, but made boots for them to protect their tender feet as they walked over the stones.' "

Each written in ink, the script obviously labored over, the letters to Mrs. Stewart express a touching warmth of gratitude, and an eagerness for the Bible to be sent; but the photographs of the men and women intent on their lessons in the schoolhouses are as moving to me as the far more professional ones by Walker Evans in James Agee's *Let Us Now Praise Famous Men,* a book about the summer in 1936 that Agee, and sometimes Evans, lived with three tenant families in Alabama. The rural people of Rowan County came to their lessons wearing their Sunday clothes—the women in blouses and skirts or long dresses, the men in suits, many with ties neatly knotted at the collars of shirts no doubt washed and ironed by their wives. Judging from the limited evidence of these pictures, more men than women attended the classes. The women tend to be in groups, some of them with infants in their laps. In the foreground of one photograph, overcoats and hats lie on a desk; the majority of the students are assembled in the front row, watching a group of four men and one woman who, under the supervision of their teacher, are solving problems in multiplication and addition on the blackboard. (The classes included lessons in arithmetic, as well as in reading and writing, and drills that covered subjects as diverse as history, civics, health and sanitation, and correct pronunciation.) On what seems to be a varnished wooden wall above the blackboard, Abraham Lincoln and George Washington look toward each other and the activity beneath the other's framed portrait.

Unlike the schoolhouse in Farmers that young Cora attended, or the descriptions of others I've come across ("Broken windows, swinging weather-boards, leaky roofs, are noticeable from without," is the way an official Kentucky document of 1871 describes a typical district school. "Inside are filthy floors, smoked ceilings, and walls defaced with obscene images."), the rooms revealed in the photographs in *Moonlight Schools* are clean and in surprisingly good repair; one picture even shows windows decorated with filmy white curtains.

From the text we learn that the introduction of the night classes for adults brought about the renovation of the Rowan County district schools by the new students themselves, and that once renovated, they became community centers for singing schools and prayer meetings, and for meetings of clubs devoted to improvements in agriculture and in roads. "The schools used to just drag along and nobody seemed interested," a trustee of one school said. "We had not had a night school but three weeks until we got together right. We papered the house, put in new windows, purchased new stovepipe, made new steps, contributed money, and bought the winter's fuel."

Reminded by these *Moonlight Schools* photographs of *Let Us Now Praise Famous Men*, I turned to Agee's discussion of rural education in Alabama, remembering some words of his about literacy, and wondering what, from his experiences among those poverty-stricken people in 1936 (the year of Cora Stewart's death), he had to say that might possibly relate to her work among the Appalachian poor. " 'Literacy,' " he writes, possibly in reference to the continuing efforts against illiteracy in Alabama that were begun in 1919 through her Rowan County example and Alabama speechmaking,

is to some people a pleasing word: when "illiteracy" percentages drop, many are pleased who formerly were
shocked, and think no more of it. Disregarding the
proved fact that few doctors of philosophy are literate,
that is, that few of them have the remotest idea how to
read, how to say what they mean, or what they mean in
the first place, the word literacy means very little even as
it is ordinarily used. An adult tenant writes and spells and
reads painfully and hesitantly as a child does and is incapable of any save the manifest meanings of any but
the simplest few hundred words, and is all but totally
incapable of absorbing, far less correlating, far less
critically examining, any "ideas" whether true or false;
or even physical facts beyond the simplest and most
visible.

The success of volunteer teachers in reducing illiteracy percentages through an ever-spreading number of
Moonlight Schools in America led to an increasing
attack on the schools by educational specialists, who,
whether Agee would find *them* literate or not, ultimately managed to take control of the movement
through arguments similar to his own about the
dubiousness of mere statistics compiled, they noted, by
nonexperts. Agee's debunking of literacy ratios,
though, was part of his criticism of education itself as
an institution—a criticism encompassing enough to
include those specialists and the Harvard of his own
undergraduate years, as well as the Cornell where I continue to teach. He was alienated enough to think of

education generally as an adjustment to a status quo that crippled rather than freed its pupils.

Agee's own prose resonates far more with the rhythms of the King James version of the Bible than does Cora Stewart's. "In every child who is born," he writes, indulging in those rhythms at the expense of conventional or even "literate" syntax, "under no matter what circumstances, and of no matter what parents, the potentiality of the human race is born again: and in him, too, once more, and of each of us, our terrific responsibility towards human life; towards the utmost idea of goodness, of the horror of error, and of God." The truly educated person would have a sharpened awareness of human potentiality, a scorn for the social authority that continually thwarts it, and a desire to accept his or her responsibility for its liberation within others. Agee's Alabama tenant farmers have had at best but a few years of education, but what does that matter, given the hopelessness of the present-day educative process? "They would be at a disadvantage if they had more of it," he says, "and at a disadvantage if they had none, and they are at a disadvantage in the little they have; and it would be hard and perhaps impossible to say in which way their disadvantage would be greatest."

Against such a view, I reread some of the lessons incorporated by Mrs. Stewart into the various publications she composed as texts—first a weekly newspaper of Rowan County events, later some readers—whereby adults could become literate with the help of teachers. Here is the first lesson of the first reader:

Can you read?
Can you write?
Can you read and write?
I can read.
I can write.
I can read and write.

A later lesson obviously supports the institutions of the day:

I shall pay my taxes.
I pay a tax on my home.
I pay a tax on my land.
I pay a tax on my cattle.
I pay a tax on my money.
I pay a tax on many other things.
Where does all this money go?

It goes to keep up the schools.
It goes to keep up the roads.
It goes to keep down crime.
It goes to keep down disease.
I am glad that I have a home to pay taxes on.

The rural poor of eastern Kentucky in Cora Stewart's time were surely as impoverished as the tenant farmers that Agee knew in Alabama, the important difference being that the mountaineers owned their own acres of clay and were proud—sometimes fiercely so—of their independence. But given the enormous disparity between them and the well-to-do in the towns and in the cities of Lexington and Louisville, the lesson encouraging them to pay their taxes, whether or not they had sufficient food or clothes for their children, would, I think, have aroused Agee's contempt, even as the pitifully small vocabulary they were gaining would, in his opinion, only have made them more susceptible to the lies and distortions that already had eroded the potentiality that had been theirs at birth.

No doubt Cora Stewart, who was as patriotic as she was religious, had a naive view of what her schools could accomplish for her pupils and hence for America. In a 1917 speech quoted by the Charlotte, North Carolina, *Observer,* she said that the newly literate adults would become "a new and powerful force promoting schools, building up trade, and swelling the avenues of religious, civic, and commercial enterprise." And she argues in *Moonlight Schools* that complete literacy in America would erase the ignorance that permits an opening for Bolshevism and other revolutionary movements antithetical to our heritage.

Whatever the inner tensions and anxieties that may have contributed to the back problems that continued to bother her after an operation at the Mayo Clinic, she had none of Agee's self-doubts, guilts, or worries about

our national moral failings. In the second year of her
Rowan County crusade, the Louisville *Courier-Journal*
reported that she "would appear at one school at the
opening to encourage the teachers and spur the students
on. Then she would mount her horse and ride over the
mountains to reach another school in time to say good-
night and tell the people how splendid they were and
how certain they were to win their battle for knowledge."

Still, the Moonlight Schools were successful in what
they set out to do, not only because of Mrs. Stewart's
energies, but because those schools so clearly were a
response to a desire within the people they served. Here
was no institution forced upon a populace, but one
whose teachers received no pay and whose students
came of their own will. Lessons on the betterment of
their communities might include the necessity of paying
taxes in order to achieve better roads and schools and to
lower the crime rate, but such lessons seem to have been
part of what the students wanted to hear. I have come
across no indication that the adults were anything but
gratified by their studies, especially by their ability to
write their own names and then to read their Bibles and
newspapers, however haltingly they might at first do so;
and to compose simply worded letters to those family
members who, in numbers that were to increase with
the burgeoning rate of literacy, had left for greater opportunities in more prosperous regions of the country.

7

Cora Wilson Stewart's mission, thwarted by the growing Great Depression and changing social attitudes, was finally taken from her hands by professional educators with less evangelical and more circumscribed proposals of their own. Toward the end of her life, the woman who had wanted to save millions from the blindness of their illiteracy became blind herself, a victim of glaucoma; but in her failing years she was nurtured—so Nelms says, relying on the testimony of one of Mrs. Stewart's relatives—by her memories of her successes as a crusader against illiteracy.

Her most sustaining memory must have been of her initial crusade in Rowan County, for it came far closer to achieving its goal than did any other in which she participated. On one of my recent visits to that county, I ran into a former student of mine who now is employed in the present literacy program; she told me that twenty-five percent, an estimate that might be conservative, of the rural residents are presently illiterate, and that teachers have difficulty first in contacting them and then in persuading them of the worth of overcoming the handicap. The Japanese car plant that has come to the Lexington area constitutes the single incentive she knows of, since a prospective employee must be able to read instructions before he or she will be considered for a job.

But in 1913, at the conclusion of the third and final

year of the campaign she led, Mrs. Stewart could find through patient canvass only twenty-three in the county who couldn't read and write. Seventeen of these, she reports in *Moonlight Schools,* were incapable of learning because of physical or mental disabilities. Of the remaining six, two had just moved into the county and the other four—the extent of her failure—simply "could not be induced to learn."

A
COUNTRY DOCTOR:
IN PURSUIT
OF HER SECRET

1

Though W. D. ("Snooks") Crutcher, proprietor and editor of the Rowan County *News* for many years, gave scant reference to such a major event as the Rowan County War in an issue devoted to the region's history, he was never one to let brevity or the objectivity claimed for his profession stand in the way of his local enthusiasms. (His boosterism was to make him an invaluable ally of Dr. Louise in her attempt to bring a hospital to Morehead.) The celebratory issue of May 10, 1956, gives more space to one family than any other —a half-page of pictures and words under the headline, "History of Caudill Family Runs Parallel to Founding and Development of County." The story's lead consists of three paragraphs, each of them insisting on the same point to such a degree that any one of them would have sufficed for a more temperate editor:

> No name in the annals of Rowan County history has come more to symbolize progress, community interest and outstanding citizenship than the name of Caudill.
>
> The Caudill family history has run almost parallel to Rowan County history. In every major enterprise since shortly after the county was founded the Caudill family name has been represented, whether it be business, civic, religious or educational.

So closely interwoven with Rowan County is the name Caudill that the two are inseparable; members of the Caudill family have been and are now leaders in the events which have marked Rowan County history.

"Caudill" is the name of so many families in eastern Kentucky that the telephone directory of almost any town contains a block of them. (The folklorist at Cornell who interviewed me in connection with my application for a job told me that the name, occasionally spelled "Caudle," is an erosion or elision of the Scotch "Caldwell," though Louise doesn't believe that this is the case: at least not for *her* particular family.) The house that Jean and I bought in Morehead was located on a lane called Caudill Court, and our property adjoined that of Cornelius P. Caudill, who then was president of the bank that issued us the mortgage. I supposed that the doctor to whom we took our young son for treatment was a distant relation of that banker, but only in the way that most Smiths or Johnsons are somehow related, which isn't much different from the biological relationships that could be shown to relate most of us, if the lineages could only be traced far enough back. While living in Morehead, I made no connection between the doctor with rooms above the jewelry store and my neighbor who ran a bank or others belonging to the most prominent family in the county.

During the years that Louise was physician to our children, both she and Susie lived with her parents in a house on Wilson Avenue (named for an earlier doctor who lived on it, Jeremiah Wilson, Cora Stewart's father), a fact I connected with her probable need to conserve funds. Knowing nothing about her parents, I thought of her as a woman with few financial resources, who had probably gone into debt to gain a medical education so that she might serve the truly impoverished. I knew she gained little recompense from her rural practice. Her reputation among the specialists in Lexington was for the modesty of her fees as well as the accuracy of her diagnoses. The Lexington obstetrician to whom Louise sent Jean—for we decided that, however much we trusted her, we wanted the birth in a hospital—let me know only minutes after Cris was born that *he* wanted more than a sack of potatoes for the successful delivery. (Thinking he was joking, I smiled, but he didn't smile back.) My pleasure many years later when I learned that Louise had managed to get a small clinic, one with a birthing room, came from my misconception that such a facility would probably have been beyond her means.

In short, I connected Louise with an ideal of poverty, one that, like St. Francis's, I could admire from a distance, since I had no desire to join the brotherhood myself. And so, when Jean and I made our first visit back to Morehead, I was as disconcerted by the house in which she and Susie now lived as by any of the other alterations that had come to the community. While far from ostentatious, it had certain amenities, such as a large enclosed swimming pool, the room containing it

opening on a terrace above a tennis court. A rambling
Florida-style bungalow, it had large living spaces; and
was set on a little hill in a parklike area of similar homes
built in what had been woods and overgrown farmland
during the years my family had lived in Morehead. (The
area carried an odd sanctity in my memory. Taking a
walk through those fields and woods on one of our final
Sundays in town, Jean and I and our young children
came upon a dilapidated barn where a man and his son
were dehorning a tightly tethered calf. Until the son
staunched the flow with grease, twin fountains of blood
rose high from the wounds, one of them falling back on
the calf's skull, matting the fur and dripping toward its
mild eyes. This image will always remain with me, not
only because the actual sight was shocking, but because
it returned me to the basement Sunday schools of my
childhood, with their pictures and lessons of a forgiving
Christ on the Cross: to a Christianity I thought I had
left behind. I found it disturbing, like an act of desecra-
tion, that the houses of suburbia had replaced those dark
woods and sunny fields become friendly through
neglect, that leaning and weatherbeaten old barn.)

On the night Jean and I knocked at Louise's door, we
thought we'd come to the wrong house and were prepared for the occupant to direct us elsewhere, simply
because of the Cadillac parked in the driveway.

To return to a town after thirty years is to perceive
some of the misconceptions that once had served to

excuse or to glorify the nature of others. Whatever the specific images that we can recall, the personality of another is remembered as a kind of emotional atmosphere, sometimes as a marvelously rich fragrance. "Louise," the current president of Morehead State University, C. Nelson Grote, is quoted as saying in a recent Louiseville *Courier-Journal* article about the achievements she has made in her seventy-five years, "can make you feel good just by transposing [to you] her own optimism and attitude. Just going to see her is kind of a renewal." His words are as valid as any verbal description can be for the feeling I had for her when, after years of absence, she returned to me in a dream. They help to account for the sense I had, as Louise invited Jean and me into her house on that night, of returning to a town and a home that always had been ours, whatever my sense of being a stranger while actually living there. That is, my memory of her nature was accurate, even though my assumptions about her background were wrong.

Since Louise is a member of that influential family whose name is "so closely interwoven with Rowan County . . . that the two are inseparable" (indeed, the now-deceased banker who issued us our mortgage was her "Uncle 'Nelius"), I give here much of the rest of the Rowan County *News* story—which makes no reference to her—for its information about her paternal antecedents, particularly about her grandfather Abel:

Samuel Caudill, grandfather of many of the present-day generation of Caudills in Rowan County, was born in Wise County, Va. in 1804. His wife, Sarah Maggard Caudill was born there in 1809.

The Samuel Caudill family moved to Troublesome Creek in Letcher County and then to Rowan County shortly after the Civil War.

Abel Caudill, their son, was a member of the Confederate Army during the Civil War. He had been born Feb. 4, 1843, in Letcher County.

Abel was married to Mary Ann Hall, on Nov. 15, 1866. They were the parents of 15 children: Robert T. and John Caudill (twins); Amanda Susan Caudill; Samuel M. and Sarah W. Caudill (twins); Emma Caudill; Lydia J. Caudill; George W. Caudill; William C. Caudill; Daniel B. Caudill; Joseph E. Caudill; David C. Caudill; Cornelius P. Caudill; Hannah M. Caudill and Watson H. Caudill.

Abel Caudill spent his entire married life in Rowan County. He raised his family on a farm at Wagoner, where he also successfully owned and operated a general store and was postmaster. He raised, bought and sold livestock, owned and operated a grist mill, flour mill and saw mill and was one of the leaders in Rowan County's commercial life.

Abel Caudill founded the Peoples Bank of Morehead in 1906 and began its operation on Jan. 1, 1907. Another of his business enterprises was the Caudill-Blair Grocery Company which he organized in 1910 and which was operated until 1932.

Caudill Cemetery, at the west corporation limits of

Morehead, was laid out by Abel Caudill after he moved in 1910 to Clearfield. It was originally intended for a family cemetery, and a family lot for each of his children was provided by him.

He left the farm at Clearfield and moved to Morehead in his declining years, and lived here until his death on July 1, 1925.

A story elsewhere in that issue summarizes the history of the Peoples Bank, and says that in founding it with others, including all of his sons, Abel "envisioned that Morehead would grow and prosper"—a faith that also led him, as I learned from local residents, to accumulate the real estate that would eventually bring much of his personal prosperity. The financial acumen of Abel and his sons became a major benefit to the community as a whole, especially during the depression years; the article about the Peoples Bank says of the bleak period in which "many banks had to close their doors," that theirs "not only remained one of the soundest banks in Kentucky, but showed increases in resources in the leanest years the nation has ever seen."

When she learned that I was thinking of writing a book that would place her within the context of her native county and its history, Louise took Jean and me almost at once to that cemetery laid out by her grandfather Abel, as if it had to be central to whatever I possibly could have in mind. We wandered about those tombstones, reading the names of her ancestors, Abel's as well as that of his wife, born Mary Ann Hall, and those of their numerous offspring, including Louise's father, named, like D. B. Logan and so many others in the region, for Daniel Boone. Daniel's grave, of course, was next to that of Louise's mother, Etta, related through the Proctor family to the Tollivers. Louise told us the story (we were to hear it again, from others in town) of the marriage of the twin brothers, Robert and John, both redheads, to another pair of redheaded twins from Morgan County, Calah and Mahalah Wells. Six children were born to these two sets of twins, and though there were no twins among *them,* they resembled each other. What a confusion of identities these two families made for others (and perhaps sometimes themselves), when they came together at social gatherings! The lives of the other twins born to Abel and Mary Ann, Louise's aunt Sarah and her uncle Sam, were destined to be almost identical in duration: driving to Sam's funeral, Sarah, along with her daughter Pearl, was killed in an automobile accident in Louisburg.

Louise likes the view from the grassy hilltop that Abel picked out for the family cemetery; from here one can not only look down on a bit of the town but across to the range of forested hills on the opposite side of the Triplett Creek valley, and to the gap in that range through which the road to neighboring Clearfield has been built. We lingered at the cemetery for maybe half an hour, not saying much, watching the sunset color the sky and the way the hills seemed to draw farther back, giving them an illusion of greater size, as evening came on. I remembered, from my years in town, how I had watched the hills move back like that, not only on summer evenings, when mists rose from them, but in fall, when the hardwoods lost their leaves.

Though she doesn't talk about the achievements of her family unless she is asked to, Louise takes pride in her grandfather Abel's ability to rise above his humble beginnings, something so many rural Rowan Countians have been unable to do, whatever the efforts of Cora Stewart and later teachers on their behalf. (Morehead State University has instituted a graduate program in social services largely because of the pressing need for trained people to process welfare applications.) When Jean asked Louise how she could account for those achievements of Abel and his descendants that separated them from so many others in the county, Louise said, "I reckon it's the genes," an answer that credited her own contributions (if she were thinking of them at all) less to herself than the family from which she had come. It was an answer, though, that would have infuriated Cora Stewart and James Agee alike. But Louise is as forthright a person as I have ever met. As a native of eastern Kentucky, she carries beneath her tolerant, unassuming, and ironically humorous outlook both a strong sense of personal independence (neither social attitudes nor the ire of the American Medical Association and its Kentucky affiliate can keep her from saying or doing whatever she feels to be right) and a loyalty to maternal as well as paternal ancestors that makes her declare of my interpretation of Craig Tolliver that there's probably another side to that particular story.

One long-time friend of hers believes that she has given herself so unselfishly to others at least partly from her knowledge of just how fortunate she and her family have been. Though the Peoples Bank of Morehead has passed from Caudill hands (the friend thinks it a shame that it didn't remain with the founding family: "Something's missing, the bank's simply not the same anymore"), Louise became president of the bank in Sandy Hook, a much smaller town in the region, upon the death of her brother Boone. His widow, Jane, and their son, B. Proctor, are the officers in charge of its daily operations. (B. Proctor, known as "Proc," was a first-grade playmate of our son, Larry, but, of course, then I was unaware of the family source of his name.)

Louise doesn't heat her swimming pool in winter, the cost striking her as exorbitant. Nevertheless, both the pool and tennis court enable her for much of the year to engage in physical activities she enjoys (she still would play tennis every day, if weather and patients permitted). Both facilities are connected to her first profession—for seven years, she was the women's physical education teacher at the college and instructed students both in swimming and in tennis.

The house itself constitutes the only bit of duplicity I've discovered in her life. Knowing that good doctors for the new hospital under construction might be hard to attract, given the smallness of the town, she built it, she says, a mischievous glint in her eyes, "to let them know the handsome fees and good life they could have if they came to Morehead." Her next-door neighbors, Judge Elijah M. ("Lige") Hogge and his wife, Norma, are two of her closest acquaintances. (Lige's paternal grandfather was Sheriff Hogg; through his mother's family, he is related to D. B. Logan as well.) Both Lige and Norma think Louise built the house where she did so that she and Susie would be able, in any late-night emergency, to care for the Hogges' two children, both afflicted with the same and finally fatal illness; but that a major reason for the *kind* of house that she put there was just as she had said, to put on a good show for all prospective surgeons and other specialists. Dr. Herbert Hudnut, a specialist in internal medicine who now practices in Glens Falls, New York, was the first director of the St. Claire Medical Center. He and his wife recall their pleasure at being wined and dined at Louise's new house, where they were offered a dip in the pool, and for the warmth of the hospitality shown them not only by Louise and Susie but by many others, such as Lige and Norma, who wanted the hospital to succeed. (Louise wasn't the only one of that group to have friends at the state capitol in Frankfort, and so Dr. Hudnut doesn't know for sure who persuaded the governor to give him the honorary title of Kentucky Colonel.)

Maybe Louise's first Cadillac was for the same, now long since successfully accomplished, cause; but the one Jean and I saw in the driveway on our first visit was not

there on our second. In her seventy-sixth year, Louise
had tired of Cadillacs, turning her latest one in for a
Mercedes "just for the fun of seeing how it would go."

2

In Morehead, as in any small town, the various
churches are central to social life, and I suppose one
reason I remained a stranger there for six years was that
I did not join, or even attend, any of them. In 1956, as I
was already preparing to leave the region, I gave no
more attention to the article about the Christian church
of Morehead in that fat issue of the Rowan County
News commemorating the county's centenary year than
I did to the article connecting that church to the beginnings of the college. The article about the Christian
church calls Inez Faith Humphrey, one of the two members of my department whose methods and courses I
had helped to displace, "a real spiritual leader" of it, and
says that the other, Gabriel Banks, frequently served as
an interim pastor.

Miss Humphrey retired a year or two after my
arrival, and I knew little about her other than that she
must have had a more than ordinary influence upon the
past generations, for each fall the entering class contained a number of young women who either had been
named by their parents for her, or whose mothers had
been so named by *their* parents. I came to know Gabriel

Banks better, for he was my colleague throughout my stay. He was a quiet and kindly person who never showed any resentment toward the usurpers, not even when the antique rolltop desk that seemed part of his personality was carted from his longtime office to the basement space he was required to share with me and others as proof that all the members of the department were comrades.

Toward the end of his career in the ministry, Gabriel had served as a missionary in India. He lent me, for a dissertation I was writing on the English novelist E. M. Forster, some books on Hinduism. Maybe in the metaphysics of that religion, he said with a smile, I would see the reason he had been unsuccessful in converting the heathens to Christianity. The strength of Hinduism, so far as he could tell from his own experiences, came from its amoebalike ability to surround and digest whatever it came across. A wealthy Brahman, for example, had invited him to dinner, listened imperturbably to his message, and then, without any alteration in his own spiritual views, had written him a large check to be used to buy Bibles for other Hindus.

I liked Gabriel for telling me that story, and I wondered if he had left the ministry for college teaching as a consequence of that and similar bafflements in India. Among the books he lent me were a pair of thick volumes, George Foot Moore's *History of Religions,* which, in their account of Buddhism as well as Hinduism, were to influence me almost as much as did my reading of

Forster's *A Passage to India*. They no doubt also contributed to that frightening sense of the illusionary nature of phenomenal reality of my older years against which, as I have said, my dreaming mind seemed to have relived the moment in which Dr. Louise, whatever the trembling of her hand, had so perfectly aligned my young son's badly torn lip that no trace of the wound remains.

Obviously, Gabriel, that occasional Christian church pastor, was a tolerant man; and one of Louise's continuing virtues is her willingness to acknowledge that another's truth may be as viable as her own. (Certainly her lack of religious bigotry helped to overcome that of others who were opposed to the establishment of a Catholic hospital in a region that continued to emphasize revivalism and a literal reading of the Gospels.) Still, when I erred in one of our discussions by referring to her Methodist upbringing, she corrected me at once; her membership in the Christian church is to her an important fact in her biography.

According to the article in the Rowan County *News,* the Morehead Christian church "is committed to the historic principles of the Disciples of Christ," and so:

The purpose of this church shall be as revealed in the New Testament to win people to faith in Jesus Christ and commit them actively to the church, to help them grow in the grace and knowledge of Christ that increasingly they may know and do His will, and to work for the

unity of all Christians and with them engage in the common task of building the Kingdom of God,

tenets that suggest its ecumenical nature. Gabriel Banks
was fulfilling the Christian church's missionary
demands in going to India. His lack of success perhaps
can be attributed to its lack of doctrinal rigidity and his
own liberalism, as well as to another religion that, in
acknowledging that each of the triad of deities it wor-
ships is ultimately an illusion whereby the adept
attempts to approach the Unknown (or so I remember
from my reading of George Foot Moore three and a half
decades ago) cheerfully accepts Christ into its pantheon.
Gabriel's predecessors in the faith, Frank Button and
Cora Wilson Stewart, dedicated themselves to Christianity with greater personal rigor, their accomplishments intimately connected with a depth of spiritual
belief that admitted no obstacle.

In renewing my acquaintanceship with Louise, my
primary desire was to uncover, like a detective of the
soul, her spiritual basis. It seemed to me from the beginning (and it still does) that Christianity, which in one
Protestant form or another has had such a deep influence
upon the region, had been of fundamental importance
to her; but when at our first real interview I tried to
explore her beliefs I found myself up against a normally
outspoken person who suddenly had become as elusive
as Dr. Godbole, the Brahman in Forster's novel. (Well,
I could understand the difficulties; as a high school grad-

uate being interviewed for a college fellowship by a quartet of professors, I could only say, "I like Christ's example, things like human brotherhood and the Golden Rule, but I don't believe in miracles" when I was bluntly asked to reveal my philosophy of life, and today probably can't do much better.)

As a member of a later generation than Cora Stewart's, Louise attended Morehead Normal only through the third grade, transferring then to the public school system; and so she was not generally subjected to a religious atmosphere in her studies beyond the degree found in public education of the day. (Rowan County's first high school was established in 1921, with five ninth-grade students constituting its enrollment. By 1924, it was a three-year high school, with only four pupils for the three grades; students over sixteen attended the normal school. The first class to complete four years at the high school was graduated in 1927. Louise was valedictorian of the class of 1930, which had nine graduating members.)

As she made apparent, nothing of the missionary or crusading spirit attaches to Louise, whatever her service to the rural poor or the effort she put into the campaign to bring a hospital to the region; nor was she drawn to medicine out of any view that such work was "in harmony with God." She ultimately became a doctor because from an early age that was what she wanted to be, and the fulfillment she has found in her profession has nothing to do with religious convictions. In a 1979

newspaper article about an honor she had just received
—a Woman of Achievement award bestowed by the
Kentucky Federation of Business and Professional
Women—she is quoted as saying that what she likes
best about her work is simply the chance it gives her for
"talking to others," a view substantiated by some of her
patients I talked to. In trying to explain the reason
everybody in her family was "just crazy about Louise,"
one woman told me, "She'll look in your two eyes and
talk to you and maybe light a cigarette, though I don't
know if she does that now." (Actually, she doesn't, but
Louise was maybe seventy before she conquered that
addiction.) To amplify what she meant by that, this
woman said that "Louise is never in a rush, you see,
and never has been," which sometimes means, she
added ruefully, that Louise gets far behind in her
appointments, much like all the doctors in town. What
sets her apart from the others is that Louise "really
wants to know all about the family."

Some residents may see a new Cora Stewart in
Louise, but she clearly doesn't. Her mother knew that
famous lady "quite well," and as a child, Louise frequently "would hear that name" at home and in school.
But Louise never considered the other woman as a role
model, even though once, following a high school
speech she had given as part of a debate, somebody
came up to her and whispered, "Another Cora Wilson
Stewart!" The remark startled her because she was in
such a panic that she couldn't remember afterward if

she had been "saying her speech or not," but guessed she had said it, since she found herself back in her seat.

Louise admits that she does not have Cora Stewart's oratorical abilities, and (except for the auditor at her school debate) I've heard of nobody who disagrees with the assessment. She'll give a talk whenever she's asked to, particularly if the subject strikes her as important; but as one member of the community remarked, she just says what's on her mind without any attempt to organize the material into a persuasive argument. ("When you say something you believe is right, I guess you don't think you need to be persuasive," Louise told me in reference to a long-ago speech to the Kentucky Medical Association that she said she had botched. It concerned certain proposals for the new Morehead hospital that the association considered socialistic and hence professionally unethical.)

Actually, the whole question of role models—whether she had one, or is one to younger women—bores her. Only two women were in her medical school class, and she was the first woman to practice medicine in Rowan County, but such statistics carry no apparent meaning for her. Judge Hogge says that, as the first woman doctor, she "surely had a little mountain to climb," but Louise doesn't see it that way. She simply set out to do what she wanted to and found it fun.

What she shares with Cora Stewart (other than an optimistic nature) is the same church and an interest in education that, despite the demands of her practice, led her to serve two terms, from 1972 until 1980, on the Kentucky Council of Higher Education as well as to head a fund-raising drive for Morehead State University. For years a deacon in her church, she is now one of its trustees—natural enough positions for her, since it was the church of her parents and the one she has attended all her life. Beyond that, the Christian church's intimate connections with the county's past are important to her. (According to the Rowan County *News* story, the present church structure stands on the site of the Union Church Building used by all of the denominations in town during the chaotic years of the Rowan County War; Frank Button, the first Christian church minister in town, of course preached from its pulpit.)

Louise's attachment to her church has much to do with the part played by the local congregation and its national organization in preparing the way for higher education in the region, and for the fact that through the years many more members of the congregation than Inez Faith Humphrey and Gabriel Banks have been affiliated with the college that developed into a university. For example, Warren Lappin, the long-standing college dean who made a majority of the curricular and staffing decisions during my tenure, not only had been the mathematics and history teacher at the normal school, but his father, like Frank Button before him, had served both as president of the normal school and Christian church pastor.

Information of this sort may reveal something about

Louise's public nature and her social attachments, but it doesn't help very much as insight into what I was after. To discover the spiritual essence of another—what an impossible task, when our own continues to elude us! Louise might drive a Mercedes and own a house with an indoor swimming pool and have had a hard time overcoming a nicotine habit while continuing to hold onto some suspect concepts about the genes of her Caudill ancestors, but clearly *something* radiated from that independent-minded little seventy-five-year-old doctor that was felt by almost everybody who came into her presence.

One evening, I called her up, as I occasionally did to clarify some aspect of her biography; I wanted to know on this occasion more about her work in education, particularly what she had done as a member of the Kentucky Council on Higher Education. We agreed with each other that anybody can waste a lot of time on councils and committees, making proposals that nobody pays much attention to—the group being appointed in the first place so that somebody in higher authority can claim he (for such authority is usually male) knows about the problem and is doing all that he can possibly do to solve it. Anyway, Louise said, you can't talk about the problems of higher education as if they existed in isolation from everything else; if she had managed anything in her eight years on the Higher Education Council, it was to get the members to think of other things—the problems of the first grade, for example. The problems begin even farther back than that, of course; all anybody can do is try to get to the beginning of them, and then do one little thing after another in the attempt to solve them. To work in such a manner might not seem like much, but she figured it was likely to do more good than anything that any recent politician in Washington had accomplished for the nation. I agreed, adding that to work in such a fashion, while refusing to admit defeat, just possibly might remedy some of the mistakes they make in Washington.

Our conversation paused. Then Louise said hesitantly, "Jim?" "What?" I asked. "Listen," she began, "I know you promised to write a book about the county that would say something about me, but if for any reason you don't want to, if you don't find it brings you whatever it is you want . . . " The sentence didn't need finishing; Louise was responding to some note of despair or frustration in my voice and wanted me to know I could wiggle off the hook of any vow I might have made without lessening our friendship.

"But I want to write this book, Louise. Do you know why?"

"Why?"

"Because it's fun. It's fun to think about, it's fun to do." Not until I used that word the third time did I remember how frequently she used it herself, as an explanation for her actions; but it was as true for me on this project as apparently it was for her in almost anything she chose to do. Just listening to that voice with its humorous and half-ironic accents, its gentle Kentucky drawl, made me realize once again how much I enjoyed its sound, and everything I had come to associate with it.

"Well, that's all right, then."

"Yes," I said.

"Good-bye."

"Good-bye, Louise."

Just as I was about to hang up, she said, again, "Jim?"

"Yes?"

"What I said about starting at the beginning, and then doing one little thing after another . . . "

"Yes, Louise?"

"Well, it's about as much as I can tell you."

"About yourself?" But that didn't need an answer: it was obvious that Louise knew what had been bothering me and was trying to tell me the answer as best she could.

"You just do it, that's all. The little things you do are mainly underneath. Sometimes it's just a kind of talking. If it's a help, especially to the little kids, it makes you a better person."

"That's the fun, I suppose."

"I reckon there's more than one kind of fun, but maybe that's the best kind."

And maybe the more abstruse the question, the simpler any conceivable answer has to be. After we hung up, I sat by the telephone, thinking that she hadn't said that the little things, mainly underneath, which we do to help others make us *feel* we are better persons, a construction most of us would accept. She had said they actually *make* us better persons, as if such small actions are as tangible as a communion wafer that the body digests, and that henceforth is held to be part of our very nature. Augustine, that fourth-century saint who knew of the importance of habit and past actions to personality and who also knew that the good act gives us happiness, would have agreed with Louise, however much he would disparage (stern figure that he was) all other kinds of fun.

———

At some level, all of us are unknowable, and I realized that such an answer was as adequate as any I could find. Still, in the following days and weeks I mulled it over, making connections between it and Agee's *Let Us Now Praise Famous Men* as well as Joseph Campbell's *The Power of Myth,* a recently published book that had brought Louise to mind. I had bought the book after hearing a rerun of Bill Moyers's televised series of interviews with Campbell—the interviews that resulted in the book.

The potentiality that Agee finds in each of us at birth, crippled or frustrated into rage and violence as it may be by society and its institutions, is linked to his view of the nature of God: to a principle of good that unifies and sanctifies everything within our universe. That is to say (if my understanding of Agee is correct), we are born with the knowledge of that principle, and were we only permitted to let it develop within us, we would have fulfilling lives. Louise, I thought, had managed better than I or the majority of us to withstand the societal pressures and hence to respond to her innate potential; the pleasure—the fun—it gave her to do so provided the radiance that others responded to, enabling them in turn to recapture something they had misplaced or lost. To my mind, her example lent the particular kind of credence that Campbell's now-famous personal exhortation to "follow your bliss" seems to need. Her example demonstrates the connection between bliss and goodness in each of us, and shows the reason that, as Campbell says, "if you follow your bliss you put yourself on a kind of track has been there all the while, waiting for you, and the life that you ought to be living is the one you are living. When you begin to see that, you begin to meet people who are in the field of your bliss, and they open the doors to you. I say, follow your bliss and don't be afraid, and doors will open where you didn't know they were going to be."

So far as I could tell, Louise's own struggle came only in the beginning, when she was afraid and unsure of her ability to do what she most wanted to do; and even here she was helped by another, a new friend who was to become her lifelong assistant and companion, Susan Halbleib.

But exactly how was it that a woman like this could

bring a major hospital, with its sophisticated and expensive array of modern diagnostic tools and its large staff of competent professionals, to a small town in the Kentucky hills? Having summarized my findings as a detective of the intangible, I will tell the rest of Louise's story as concretely and objectively as I can, so that it can stand as part of a historical record that includes the Rowan County War and the achievements of Cora Wilson Stewart. The drama is ultimately that of the community itself.

THE COMING OF
ST. CLAIRE
TO MOREHEAD

1

Claire Louise Caudill was born August 19, 1912. Her mother, Etta, was, Louise says, "little," and her father, Daniel, "big." (By "big" she apparently doesn't mean "stout," but rather that he had a tall and imposing presence. In group photographs I have seen—for example, one with family members, another with a civic group of which he was a member—he stands near the back, but the viewer's attention is drawn to him.) According to the family story, Daniel was infatuated with the beauty of Etta, as demure as she was diminutive, and persisted in the courtship despite her denials and hesitancies. The marriage turned out to be a good one; Louise remembers a stable and affectionate family environment. She was the second to be born; "there were two boys, two girls, and one [Louise herself] tomboy."

Upon the marriage of his children, Abel Caudill, Daniel's father, normally gave them five hundred dollars; but Daniel and one of his brothers, William, persuaded Abel to let them have the money before marriage, to help them through college. Both sons studied law at Valparaiso University, in northwestern Indiana; Daniel became the first practicing attorney in Morehead to have a law degree. In addition to his major responsibilities, which included a long term as president of the family bank, Daniel for many years was an officer and principal stockholder of the smaller bank in Sandy Hook, and at the time of his death at eighty-seven remained its president—the position now held by Louise. Twice elected as circuit judge of Rowan and neighboring counties, he also served terms as city and county attorney and was a regent of Morehead State Teachers College. He was the son to achieve a statewide professional renown while still managing to emulate the material achievements of his father. According to the article in the local newspaper reporting his death, Daniel "was one of Morehead's largest land owners," his properties including "valuable land under lease near Morehead State University. Through the years Mr. Caudill rarely sold a piece of property once he gained fee simple title."

Boone was the son who followed him in both law and banking careers; the other son, Milton, became a dentist in Frankfort and now lives in Monticello, a small town near Cumberland Lake in the southern part of the state. An elderly woman who had lived next door to Dan and Etta's first home on Main Street, told me that on the night of Boone's birth she was awakened by Etta's screaming—"the most terrible sound I ever heard"—for Boone was born without an arm. He is the only one of the five children not still living.

If the sons were encouraged by their parents to enter suitable professions, the three daughters, chiefly under the tutelage of their mother, were expected to be "ladies," that is, young women with tact and grooming who would find husbands who came from respectable families and had decent prospects.

Lucille, the oldest of the children, and Patricia, the youngest, both became ladies in Louise's view; Patricia, who is divorced, now lives in Fort Lauderdale, Florida, and Lucille is married to a Lexington horse breeder. "Now isn't she a real lady?" Louise said admiringly to me, upon showing me a picture of her smartly dressed older sister.

Daniel seems to have been an indulgent father, sending his children to private schools of their choice (Louise says she was the only one not to go to a "fancy" school unless that word applied to Breckinridge, a grade school once connected to the college, which she briefly attended before returning to the Morehead public school system). He also paid their way through college. The five hundred dollars Abel had given Daniel was the only support he received while studying law, which meant he'd had to find odd jobs and live frugally as a student; he didn't want his children to face similar hardships. (Lucille was the one to test his indulgence through an apparent frivolity toward her studies that sent her from college to college; she attended eleven schools before she got her degree. Her example made Daniel tell Louise she'd have to stay put in whatever school she entered as a freshman, if she expected family assistance to continue.)

Louise may always have dreamed of becoming a doctor, but she feels that she easily might not have become one, for her mother, determined as always that her daughters not only grow up to become ladies, but never to give their attention to anything other than "lady things," considered medicine a highly inappropriate field for a woman. As a girl, Louise was forbidden to ride a bicycle. In high school, she enjoyed physical activity and, despite her small stature, was a good basketball player, but her mother forebade her to play on the girls' basketball team. (She was on the debating team, and that, to her mother, was the extent to which a girl should engage in competitive activities with other children.) Louise was a spectator during a basketball game that the Morehead High School girls' team was losing, and the coach said that she simply *had* to play, if Morehead were to win; and so Louise disobeyed her mother by putting on her uniform and playing in the second half.

"Did your side win?" I asked her, when she told me this story.

"I don't remember which side won," she said. "All I remember afterward was that I went against Mama's orders."

While Jean and I were staying with Louise and Susie during one of our visits to Morehead, they had a dinner party for us. The other guests were their neighbors Judge Elijah Hogge and his wife, Norma; and Bob Bishop. Jean and I had known him in the nineteen fifties as the owner of the drugstore in town where we purchased not only the Sunday *New York Times* (on the following Tuesday) but brand-name antibiotics for our cocker spaniel. Bob would sell them to us for less than half the price, so long as we promised to take none of the pills ourselves. Like Lige, Bob is a lifelong resident of Morehead, but his friendship with Louise predates Lige's.

Except for a sewing class he couldn't bring himself to take, Bob was never separated from Louise in studies from the first grade through high school. In the evenings, they did their homework together. As members of the high school debating team, they practiced their speeches before each other and went by bus and train for debates elsewhere in eastern Kentucky. Bob was salutatorian of the graduating class of which Louise was valedictorian. It was to Bob that Louise spoke of her earliest desires of becoming a doctor; he, on the other hand, told her he wanted to become a pharmacist who would fill the prescriptions she and the other local doctors ordered for their patients. But during Bob's senior year in high school, his father, proprietor of a drugstore since 1896, died; Bob and his sister Roberta had to take over the family business before he could study pharmacy. Roberta was the one who eventually became a pharmacist; Bob ran the business with a hired pharmacist while Roberta was studying for her license.

Upon *her* graduation, Louise took a job at her father's bank, just to see if the banking profession might be to her liking. "If I'd stayed, I believe I could have made a bundle in that line of work," Louise told me. "Daddy set me to sorting checks, things like that. I lasted four days before I got so bored I just had to quit."

But she was determined on a career, not on the marriage that her mother had in mind. If Louise were going to be a spinster, Etta thought that teaching was the only suitable occupation. With that goal in mind, Louise (after a semester at the local institution, which apparently her father didn't count in his injunction to her to stay put in whatever undergraduate school she entered) went off to college—to Ohio State, where she majored in physical education, a field that Daniel convinced a reluctant Etta was appropriate enough for one of Louise's aptitudes and interests. Upon her graduation in 1934, she returned to Morehead as the women's physical education teacher at the college while continuing to live at home. In summers, she attended Columbia University, securing, in 1936, the master's degree in education she would need if she were to devote her lifetime to teaching.

Louise remained a teacher at the college until 1943. "Daddy," Louise said, "saw at last I really wanted to be a doctor. He said, 'You can be anything you want to be,' and of course Momma always agreed to everything that he agreed to." And so she gave up teaching to enter the University of Louisville Medical School. The only other woman in her class is now a psychiatrist in Manhattan; Louise, loyal to her home community, never wanted to practice anywhere but in Rowan County, which, as a region without much wealth, had never attracted enough physicians to meet the demand for medical services.

I've heard it said that by the time we become seventy the memories we hold most strongly are either of very recent events or of those from our childhood; the long middle years blur into each other, and nothing much from them is recalled in detail. Such a generalization may be based on extensive research, but it doesn't apply to all of us, and it doesn't seem to have the slightest application to Louise. Whatever my questions to her, I was unable to discover much about her years of childhood and adolescence. She recalls the family warmth, but when I asked for details she could provide only the example of the bridge games she had played on weekends with her parents—and it turned out that these memories were from visits home during her college days! Perhaps the very security of her childhood years keeps them buried from recall, except for such memories as I have already presented. And it seems to me that she began to live with intensity—that is to say, with fun —only after she began the practice of medicine, with Susan Halbleib as a nurse and a partner. She was in her midthirties when she truly began to live the kind of life that as a child she had confided to Bob Bishop she dreamed of, and her memories from this point on are the strong and detailed ones.

Susie is a better cook than Louise, and so she prepared the meal for the party at which Jean and I, Lige

and Norma, and Bob were the guests. It was a congenial affair, as warm (I thought) as any bridge game
Louise might have played with her parents and one of
her brothers or sisters when she was a young woman.
In the previous year, Bob had retired from the drugstore. Though it did a fine business (following the
demise of the Eagles' Nest restaurant, it became the
chief social center on Main Street), he had decided to
close it rather than sell it to a chain, for he couldn't bear
to see it turn into something unlike what it had been for
generations. In his midseventies he no longer wanted to
work twelve hours or longer a day, seven days a week;
he had locked the door for the last time one night, and
that was that.

Cokes at his fountain had been a nickel when we
lived in Morehead, and (according to an old newspaper
account I had seen) they had still been a nickel in 1979;
I asked him if he had continued to charge five cents for
a Coke until the end, and he said—rather reluctantly—
that yes, this was so. He now owned a farm outside of
town and was doing a pretty fair job of cattle-raising,
winning prizes and so on. This was just the latest of the
many things he had done with his life; still, he figured
that after he was gone he would be remembered only as
a druggist too stubborn to raise the price of a glass of
carbonated water flavored with a special syrup.

I had liked Bob when we lived in Morehead, and I
liked him now. Except for an increased girth and hair
somewhat thinner and streaked with silver, he seemed

much the same. Though generally more quiet than Louise, he has much of her tolerant and sometimes self-deprecating humor. Actually, they have come to resemble each other somewhat, at least in physique, for both are short and Louise is a bit stockier now herself. Both possess the same stubborn resilience. At the dinner party, the talk was all of present-day events; Lige and Bob alike told some funny local stories I thought I would remember, but don't. (I didn't learn at that dinner party of Bob and Louise's close companionship throughout their public school days, but rather discovered it from a number of old acquaintances of both, as well as from accounts in the newspaper.) Like Louise, Bob has never been married. Their affection for each other is that of brother and sister, intimate enough to read and approve of much of what goes on in the other's mind.

We drank wine with Susie's meal, and sat talking for hours afterward. It was a fine dinner party.

2

Susan Halbleib, Dr. Louise's nurse, was born on March 12, 1926, and so is more than thirteen years younger than Louise. They became acquainted in late fall of 1947 at Oneida Maternity Hospital, a state-run facility in a then hard-to-reach Clay County community on the Red Bird River in southeastern Kentucky.

Susie, who has three younger brothers and one younger sister, was born in Louisville, to a Catholic family. Both grandparents on her father's side were born in Germany, though they first met in Louisville, where they were married. Her maternal grandparents came from Ireland. Susie says her parents died "too early": her father shortly after his forty-seventh birthday, her mother when she was sixty-four. Two of her brothers have retired, but the third continues to work at the Louisville General Electric plant. Her sister is a homemaker.

One of her aunts told me that Susie's desire to be a nurse apparently came while she was still a toddler barely able to talk. She would point at an adult's leg and, declaring it was "bruk," would wrap bandages around it. The aunt remembers that once Susie diagnosed a leg of the dining room table as "bruk," and carefully bandaged it, too.

Her family, Susie remarks, was "a normal, hardworking one"; while everybody was "literate enough," education was never stressed, and she was the only child to study beyond high school, and thus the only one to have a professional career. She attended Catholic schools in Louisville. Following her graduation from the Ursuline Academy in 1944, she entered Nazareth (now Catherine Spaulding) College, to study nursing, and did her clinical training at St. Joseph's Hospital; both institutions are in Louisville. Upon completion of her training at St. Joseph's, Susie had been too young

for certification as a registered nurse, and came to
Oneida—one of the few places that would hire her
before certification—as a public health nurse in maternity cases. She received certification during her stay at
Oneida.

Louise did her internship in Philadelphia at the hospital of Woman's Medical College of Pennsylvania, following her graduation in 1946 from the University of
Louisville Medical College. She is frank about all her
doubts and fears as a student and new doctor. In one of
her first classes at the medical college, "four fellows left
when they opened the lids on some cadavers," never to
return to their studies; Louise, though she felt the desire
to leave with them, had a stronger desire to "stick it
out." Soon after her arrival at the Philadelphia hospital,
she was "handed a scalpel" and told "to open up the
belly" of a patient on the operating table. "I thought I
would drop dead," she told me. "I had never done such
a procedure and really didn't know how."

"Did you do it?" I asked.

"Of course not," she said.

She remained at Woman's Medical College for
slightly more than a year. Here she became acquainted
with a woman doctor from mainland China, Hai Mai
Chen, who had come to the United States to learn Pap
smear techniques; Dr. Chen, Louise says, was "big in
OB," being head of the obstetrics department at Shanghai University Medical School. The Chinese doctor
"took on" Louise at Woman's Medical, becoming a

friend as well as a mentor. Like interns everywhere, Louise "worked around the clock, hoping for a catnap now and then," glad to gain the experience necessary for private practice. But the thought of that private practice still frightened her: "You're doing all these things in the hospital, but then you think you've got to do it by yourself later on, with no protection. There's going to be nobody else but you—the thought scares you. You've got to know what to do when something unexpected happens." Realizing that much of her work would be in obstetrics, Louise decided to gain more experience in that field before opening her own practice. She accepted the job at Oneida Maternity Hospital because the woman doctor on the staff not only "wanted somebody to come and help her," but promised to teach her "all of this big stuff" she still needed to know.

To Louise, it seemed an ideal situation. "It was a tiny hospital," she remembers, "but had everything you wanted, and you could imagine that from everything you could learn there you would be able to deliver a baby at home." Susie was one of the four nurses at the time of Louise's arrival, and there were a number of nurse's aides as well. The nurses administered anesthesia. Small as it was, the hospital had a registered dietician. Everybody "had to work hard," but that was the way Louise liked it.

The staff doctor, though, had misled Louise. The doctor was working on her state board examinations and was looking more for a substitute than an assistant. She would disappear soon after Louise came on duty and be gone for most of the day. Then she took a vacation, leaving Louise in charge. Though not required to do so, Louise, in addition to caring for the hospital patients, felt an obligation to respond to emergency calls in the county. Susie offered to pack her bag for the first of these calls; almost at once, they became a medical team.

The responsibility Louise had to assume turned out to be what she needed. The brief stay in that remote hamlet of Oneida (accompanied by Susie, Louise was to leave by the first of the year) was crucial to her, making her "feel grown-up." There was nobody to defer to; not even the husbands of the wives about to give birth could be consulted in case a quick decision had to be made. The husbands in that rural region customarily considered their duty at an end when they arrived with their wives at the hospital door, and they returned only after they had a washed and diapered son or daughter to admire.

"It's important to get not only the training, but the belief in yourself," Louise told me more than once, adding that her new association with Susie had much to do with her growing self-confidence. It is a compliment that Susie, with a disarming frankness of her own, acknowledges to be true enough.

The two stayed up late each night, reading medical books to know how to treat each of the patients they had, trying to become informed on every physical problem that they encountered or anticipated.

"You were still doing that the first time we saw you, when we brought Larry to your office," I said, when Louise told me that.

"We do it to this day," she said. (Judge Hogge later told me that he was impressed by how Louise in her mid-seventies keeps up with medical advances, studying all the latest journals and books; when Louise took Jean and me to see her clinic, she showed us her desk, littered with publications that her busy schedule had not yet given her time to examine.) Of course, patients and parents don't get in on the studying so much anymore, Louise explained, because today she is more experienced with the kind of diseases that you can easily find described in a general medical text.

Louise and Susie both enjoy reminiscing about their experiences at Oneida, and take turns filling in details about untoward events that had happened to them there. One evening, a midwife who had just delivered a baby at home phoned Louise to say that the afterbirth somehow had been retained within the mother's womb and she didn't know what to do. Louise told the midwife to bring the woman to the hospital, even though she herself "knew no more what to do than a jack rabbit." But she and Susie turned to their books; and by the time the midwife, holding the newborn baby, arrived with the mother and all the other members of the family, Louise and Susie "had learned our lesson."

Still, it was an unnerving moment for the relatively inexperienced doctor. Acting as "knowledgeable" as they could, she and Susie "got the mother all draped up" and onto the table.

The family lived in the country and apparently had never been in a hospital before. Louise said, "It was a real thrill to them to be bringing somebody in, and I reckon they had been shaking the mother around, getting her to the hospital." Apparently, all the tossing about had caused the placenta to break loose from whatever had been holding it within the womb. In any event, it came out of its own accord while Louise, her hand on the woman's belly, was considering her next move.

Sometimes, though, the patients weren't so obliging in resolving a problem for themselves, and sometimes the books gave no clear answers. Susie said that at Oneida she and Louise "learned just to wait, if you didn't know what else to do." She had done a lot of waiting there, she told Jean and me, "just sitting by the patient to see what would happen. If she delivers, at least you're there, even if you don't know what to do."

In response to that remark, Jean asked Susie a natural enough question: "But what if something abnormal happened?"

Susie replied, "I had learned enough from the books to know if something really tragic was going to happen," an event that apparently never took place. "I didn't know much about the normal process, really.

How long does labor take? It never takes the same amount of time. But I didn't think anything abnormal could happen with me sitting there."

What a serene sense of assurance for a newly licensed nurse, twenty-one years of age! I transcribed those words of hers from an early interview taped on an old recorder Jean and I had found in our house; not much more than a toy, it might have been left on a shelf long ago by a friend of one of our children. It hummed, and a soft voice like Susie's was blurred and often indistinct. Had my transcription been inaccurate? I bought an expensive recorder, one with an omnidirectional microphone, for our return visit, and asked Susie if she indeed had said that at Oneida she believed nothing abnormal could happen to a woman in labor, as long as she was sitting at that woman's side.

"Why, yes, that's exactly how I felt," Susie said. She is a slender woman, maybe five feet six in height, and her bearing is both erect and somehow tranquil. Like Louise, she has a fine sense of humor, and a gentleness of response, but unlike Louise's, her voice carries no self-irony. "I guess you're surprised at first by how much you learn and can do. But I felt I could do anything almost right away." It took her some years of nursing experience to realize that she hadn't been quite so competent in Oneida as she had felt herself to be, but she guessed it was the feeling of competence, then and as well as now, that always managed to keep her calm and collected.

In 1957—the year after Jean and I had moved from Morehead—an article about Louise's competence, as well as her dedication to medicine, appeared in the Louisville *Courier-Journal*. In that article, one of her patients is quoted as saying, "All you have to do is believe in God and that woman doctor, and so help me, you'll live forever." As was apparent from our first visit to her office, she is far more concerned about an accurate diagnosis than an outward show of expertise—an indication of the professional integrity that has imparted confidence in her abilities to thousands of her patients. That very integrity, though, must have made her apprehensive about her lack of experience when she was thrust into the position of major responsibility at Oneida; and so Susie's confidence in herself as a nurse was from the beginning a kind of spiritual bulwark for her.

When I asked Louise and Susie at the long, second interview how important each one was to the other, Louise said simply, "We couldn't do it [everything they have accomplished, as well as what they're still doing] without the other," and Susie said, "I doubt that we could have done it. Louise thinks more than I do, but I work a lot."

Louise said that yes, Susie was willing to work very hard, and took responsibility even better than she herself did. "Susie," she said, "makes *me* work."

Louise's ability to think, Susie went on, was apparent long ago, "when measles were popular." Instead of assuming that a patient had measles because he or she had a rash, Louise would look for other symptoms as well, since other diseases can cause a similar rash. Louise agreed she was a thinker, if a thinker was one who didn't jump to the most obvious conclusion. "It's true enough I don't go the easy road," she said. "I go around the perimeter."

Both of them dislike certain tendencies in modern medicine. Louise said that despite the assistance provided by Medicare and Medicaid, "having greenbacks makes more of a difference than ever in patient care." As an illustration of Louise's remark, Susie said that before Medicaid a doctor could make a call to the county judge and get an indigent patient admitted to the proper hospital right away, for the judge would immediately allocate the funds, but that "now there is much more red tape."

Keeping records has always been important to medicine, Louise said, but the increase in bureaucracy "has made paper business a good business in itself"; their small clinic, for example, now has two assistants, mainly just to keep up with the paperwork. (Not liking its impersonality, they have resisted the introduction of a computer into their clinic, though they realize that medical students now learn about computers as part of their course work and come to consider them as necessary to their practice as any other instrument.)

Too, the refusal of governmental programs to cover the cost of house calls helps to account for their precipitous decline. Even if they're not necessary from a strictly medical standpoint, such calls can have a crucial psychological value. If a patient is dying of cancer at home, treated with nothing but drugs to ease the pain, no program will pay a doctor to drop by to see that patient, however comforting that call might be to the person or his family. (Did Louise and Susie still make such calls? Yes, whenever they possibly could.)

Susie began to talk about the advertising used by modern doctors. "They advertise what they do and how much they charge," she began, but her aversion to this publicity was such that she gave up talking about it, summarizing her feelings with a guttural exclamation, an "ach!" she must have learned as a child from her German grandparents.

Louise said to her, "I believe you're more adamant toward medicine today than I am." Susie replied, "Yes, you tend to go with the flow more than I do," but it was a simple observation, not an accusation. And then both of them declared that, whatever their reservations, medicine in the United States remains better than it is anywhere else in the world.

For more than forty years, Louise and Susie have lived and worked and taken vacations together, and so have spent far more time in each other's company than have Jean and I or any other couple of our acquaintance. For a relationship to survive such intimacy, one might assume the pair would need to merge, becoming almost a single self. Louise and Susie are alike in certain respects. Both are frank and devoid of pretense. Louise may be more talkative, but Susie has an equal friendliness. As doctor and nurse in a rural practice, they have cheerfully undergone physical hardships of a sort that many medical practitioners have never faced; theirs is an identical idealism of service to humanity.

But their personalities are distinct. Tranquil and self-assured as she might seem, Susie is probably less able to control her temper; not only is she the one more angered by present-day medical tendencies, but she admits to "stepping on Louise's toes more than Louise steps on mine." Louise agrees this is probably true, though she adds that if anybody *really* steps on her toes, "Brother, you've got something!" Religion may play no part in either's attitude toward her profession, but Susie's Catholicism is as personally important to her as Louise's membership in the Christian church is to her. And as I have indicated, Susie never to my knowledge looks upon herself with the irony that seems crucial to Louise's outlook. The handyman and gardener who looks after their property has his own insight into their differences. "Dr. Louise doesn't pay attention to anything in the yard but the trees," he told me. "As for Susie, her eyes are always on the flowers."

One has to take Louise's humorous and self-scoffing irony into account in assessing her remarks about how "scared" she was as a neophyte doctor, and possibly even about her timidity in opposing her mother's expectations. (The same irony toward herself probably

accounts for her remark to me—maybe a half-truth—
that she returned to Morehead to establish her practice
because "it was the only place I wasn't scared to go.")
Still, it strikes me as likely enough that the independence of spirit I admire in Louise came at least in part,
however paradoxical it may seem, from the increasing
closeness of her relationship with Susie. The mutual
understanding and support provided by certain lucky
attachments (here I generalize from nothing but my
own marital experience) can free us sufficiently to be
ourselves and to achieve whatever it is that we want to
make of our lives. A liberation can come from the very
choice of partner that we make.

In the late winter of 1947, Louise asked Susie to come
to Morehead with her, to help her establish a practice
there; Susie, who, except for those months "way out in
the sticks" at Oneida, had never lived in a small town,
"decided to come to Morehead for at least six months
even if it killed me."

And so, during their last weeks at Oneida, they
began to gather the equipment they would need for
their Morehead office, ordering everything, Louise
says, "from a salesman who came through." Lacking
experience in what they would need, Louise purchased
an absurd number of ammonium chloride pills—one
hundred thousand of them. "Shoot," she said, remembering. "That was the strongest drug we had, a diuretic,
no longer in use. But when you know you're going out
there, into the country, you also know you've got to

give the people *something*. That drug surely lasted us, I can tell you."

Thus armed, they set off together for Morehead, to establish the practice that was to far outlast even such a stockpile of pills.

3

Not only did Louise's parents welcome Susie as well as their daughter into their house on Wilson Avenue, but Louise's father provided the office space for the practice (he owned that building on Main Street) and her mother helped Susie scrub and paint the rooms. Louise didn't join them in this chore; her mentor from her Philadelphia days, Dr. Chen, was now in New York City, and Louise wanted to see her again in this brief period of freedom before the office opened.

I was surprised to hear that Etta had adjusted herself so well to Louise's new profession that she would scrub and paint with Susie. "I thought Etta believed that women should do only what Louise calls 'lady-things,'" I said to Susie, when she told me about the work she and Louise's mother had accomplished together. She and I were talking at the kitchen table at Louise and Susie's house one Sunday morning after breakfast; Louise and Jean had gone off somewhere.

Apparently what Etta felt to be suitable for her daughters wasn't exactly what she felt necessary for herself. "Etta was pretty, and liked to dress up," Susie said. "She didn't like to keep house, but she enjoyed painting rooms, things like that." And whatever her earlier objections, her daughter had now become a doctor, and Etta, with her concern for propriety, wanted the new office to look as handsome as possible. "We made that space really shine," Susie said, taking some umbrage at some comments of mine about the way it looked the first time I saw it. "That couch you thought so decrepit . . . well, here, look at it," and she marched me into an adjoining room to see a neatly tailored couch. "We brought it home when we built the clinic and had it reupholstered. It seemed in such bad shape to you because a patient's father—" and here she paused, until she could remember both the name of the child and the father—"had burned a hole in it with his pipe, maybe only a week or so before you brought Larry in." (Both Louise and Susie have a phenomenal recall, not only of the names of patients treated thirty or more years before, but of the nature of their illnesses; Susie's memory of dates surpasses Louise's, and it was from Susie that I learned the birthdates of all of Louise's siblings.)

When Louise began her practice in late January of 1948, she had newly painted walls and a fine-looking couch; all that she lacked were patients. "Not much happened for the first few days," she admitted to Jean and me. "What we did mainly was to eat banana splits and chocolate sundaes, brought up from Bob Bishop's pharmacy." She mentioned the name of the first patient and told us of that patient's subsequent life—her marriage to a navy man, her departure to California, the divorce.

It wasn't long before Louise and Susie had to augment the few chairs in the office with others on the landing space outside the second-floor door, and soon people were waiting, as Jean and I remembered doing, on the steps leading up to it.

Louise had bought a gray 1947 Pontiac (the car she still was driving when I lived in Morehead) for her house calls, but it wasn't adequate for the muddy or snow-covered roads that led back into the hills, to the cabins where, especially in the first decade of their practice, she and Susie delivered so many babies.

(I know something of those dirt roads from weekend trips I took with my family, just to see what the back country was like: occasional cabins next to a stream in a hollow, some of the cabins without glass in the windows, most of them without electricity, children playing next to a washtub on the porch. Even on a sunny summer's day, a car could get mired in low areas, or get its differential hump caught on a boulder between the ruts. The twisting roads, some of them barely altered from the cart trails they once had been, intersected with so many others just like them that a driver not born to the area could lose any sense of direction. Once, less than ten miles from town, I became lost and asked a man sitting on a porch step if he could tell me how to get back to Morehead. He shook his head. "Never be-en thar," he said.)

Often Louise and Susie would meet the husband of a woman in labor at a predetermined point, the point beyond which no car could safely go. The man would have a horse or a mule (if the terrain was particularly difficult, a team of animals), sometimes attached to a wagon, but more frequently to a flat-bottomed sled, for such sleds could traverse mud as well as snow far better than a wheeled vehicle could. The doctor and nurse would transfer their medical equipment to the sled. "It made a burdensome amount," Susie told Jean and me, for they always took along everything they might possibly need: in addition to their medical bags, a portable delivery table, which could be unfolded and placed upon a bed; bottles and other equipment for intravenous fluids; sterile pads, and so on.

The first maternity case to take them back into the hills coincided with a heavy snowfall. On Jean's and my initial return to Morehead, Louise and Susie told us about that day, but I found a fuller account of it in the 1957 *Courier-Journal* article:

> Kentucky had just had a record snowfall on Feb. 2, 1948, when she [Louise] and Susie Halbleib . . . were summoned to a home far back in the hills.
>
> The girls [in 1957, a female doctor in her mid-thirties and a nurse of voting age still could be called that] were clad in two pairs of pajamas, slacks, fur-lined shoes, and

sheepskin-lined jackets. They drove as far as they could go by car, then were met by a man [in this case, apparently not the husband] driving two horses hitched to a crude wooden sled.

The doctor and the nurse climbed aboard and glided back into the snowy hills. They arrived at the one-room shack a little past midnight. The only heat came from a tiny drum stove.

Beside the expectant mother there were the husband, an old woman, and two small children, one of whom was very ill.

As Susie had learned at Oneida, the length and difficulty of labor is never the same; on this and all later rural calls, of course, she had Louise as a companion while waiting. They would pass the hours in tidying up a place, in talking, and in reading (when the oil lamps provided enough illumination). On this first trip into the hills, they had the sick child to attend to, as well as the mother; as they were to discover, they often had to give medical assistance to more members of a family than the one to whose bedside they had been summoned. On occasion, they attended to more than one family on any sojourn into a given neighborhood. On their first excursion, they successfully delivered the baby at noon the following day.

If that first trip can represent all such trips in snow, another can represent a number of their sloggings through mud. In this case, Louise and Susie, unable to reach their destination by car because of the mire, were met by a husband who had no sled; perhaps he was too poor to afford the horse or mule to pull one. Upon slogging to the house with him, they discovered the woman was having the baby prematurely and was hemorrhaging. They did what they could to stem the flow, but knew they would have to get her quickly to the nearest hospital. Louise and Susie, with help from the husband, carried her in a blanket to the car through two fields.

"We carried her a good mile, through fields knee-deep in mud," Louise says of the incident she remembers as the most physically exhausting of her career. Nevertheless, in telling the story, she smiles; for although the baby for some days suffered from "all these things that most premature newborns have," both mother and child "did all right."

That September, Dr. Chen came to Morehead before returning to China to be of whatever help she could in the new practice of her friend and protégée. She stayed for a month or two, accompanying Louise on her house calls. Finally, her visa having expired, Dr. Chen flew back to Shanghai, leaving Louise and Susie to their own resources. (Shortly before she departed, Louise's niece, the daughter of Boone and Jane, secretly wrote the State Department, begging that Dr. Chen be permitted to stay, saying that the region had a real need for her services. Louise found out about the letter only after an FBI agent arrived in Morehead to check up on the background of one Susan Caudill, who just might be engaging in Maoist subversion in Rowan County. Upon learning that Susan was in the second grade, he left.)

Meanwhile, Louise's practice in town continued to expand. If people were too sick to come to them during office hours, she and Susie went to their homes. One of her longtime patients remembers the winter day—"it was snowing, horribly"—that she became suddenly feverish from what turned out to be an infection. Her son called Louise's home phone number; Susie answered. Much to the surprise of both son and mother, Susie, instead of saying Louise would come to the house, suggested that he bring his mother to the office later in the day. The son said his mother was far too sick to leave the house in such weather, but Susie remained reluctant to commit Louise to a house call. "My son really got mad," the woman told me. "He shouted into the phone, 'All of our lives we've doctored with Louise, and now that my mother needs her, you can't come down!' Susie actually hung up on him, something you can't imagine she would ever do. But then she called back, saying they would be there as soon as they possibly could . . . Well, I'll have you know they *did* come, and only a few minutes later."

"Did you ever find out why Susie acted like that?" I asked.

"Yes," the woman said. "While they were here, I asked Louise about her mother, knowing that she was ill, and she said, 'Well, she died.' It had just happened, you see." I think it made this patient, now an elderly

woman, feel better to tell me this story. "Louise has
done many things like that for many people, all her
life," she went on. "No matter what, she'll come any-
time. Last night, my brother-in-law died. During his
illness, she kept coming, lots of times without being
called; she'd stop by on her way home for the night.
She's so tender and kind and all that. She'll go down in
the history of Rowan County as one of the great doctors, I know."

4

In the early 1950s, a bakery opened for business in
Morehead, a memorable event: none had existed in
town until then, and this particular bakery was run by
two sisters who made marvelous rolls, bread, and pastries. They were in their later years; for decades they
had dreamed of such a business together, and finally had
found the time and courage to undertake its operation.
The line before their counter was as long as the one on
the staircase to Louise's office; indeed, much like the
line awaiting to enter a theater for a popular movie, it
sometimes extended down the block. But they closed
the business only two or three weeks after opening it,
as I discovered the afternoon I came to buy coffee cake
for Sunday breakfast. Later, I heard they had been tear-
ful on the last day of their business, and they had apol-
ogized to the waiting customers for running out of

everything they had baked that morning. The business had succeeded so far beyond their expectations and their energy that they were too exhausted to carry it on.

Good baked goods were a luxury in that small town, but good medical care was a necessity; Louise and Susie, who often must have been as exhausted as those sisters, couldn't quit, even had they wanted to. The clinic that had been *their* dream at the time I left Morehead was a way of coping with their own physical inability, given the increasing demands made upon them, to continue those time-consuming trips into the rural areas. But they wanted the women to come to the clinic for reasons that went beyond matters of time and the limits of their own endurance. A dark and crowded cabin in the hills was hardly the most sanitary place to deliver a child; and as their experience with the woman who was hemorrhaging and in premature labor showed, the lives of both mother and infant could be endangered by a birth in such an isolated location.

And so, in 1957, ten years after Louise and Susie had met in Oneida, they opened their clinic on Main Street; it had a delivery room, two labor rooms, an X-ray room, an office, a waiting room, and a small living area for Louise and Susie. They had left the Caudill family home to live in the clinic so that one or the other, if not both, would be available night and day to attend to the women in labor.

In planning the clinic, Louise had recognized that a hospital was what the region really needed, not only for emergencies, but for laboratory work. (The lack of professional laboratory facilities in the town, she says, caused her to be especially scrupulous as a diagnostician. From the beginning of her practice she had X-ray equipment, but the film had to be forwarded to a radiologist elsewhere in the state, and no local facilities existed for the examination of blood and other specimens.) But to establish a good hospital seemed to her at that time "just too way out an idea," and the clinic at least "something I could live with."

As a birthing center, the clinic was available to all women, regardless of their ability to pay, but with the requirement that they schedule visits before labor for prenatal care. Louise and Susie hoped through the new institution to change the casual rural attitudes toward childbirth. (According to a 1988 feature story about Louise and Susie in the local newspaper, Susie "acted as disciplinarian in setting up standards to be followed at the clinic," and was "strict" in enforcing the rule about prenatal visits. This suggests that, whatever her belief that nothing abnormal could happen as long as she was in attendance, she preferred to take no chances.)

Birthing centers have become popular in recent decades as an option for women who don't want to enter a hospital; but the pioneer one in Morehead came into being simply because no hospital was available then. I asked Susie if state or national codes concerning a facility like theirs existed in 1957. "We knew we had to shield the X-ray machine from the delivery room," she said. "And we knew that for health reasons there couldn't be an air conditioner in that room. But as for codes about operating a birthing center—well, there couldn't have been any. If there had been, they surely wouldn't have permitted us to do what we did, the two of us living twenty-four hours a day in the clinic and grabbing sleep and a bite to eat whenever we could."

Though the opening of the hospital only six years later was a far more significant occasion for them and the whole community, they remember the happiness they felt on the day they celebrated the completion of the clinic. "We had a big party, an open house," Louise told me. "Lots of people came, and they brought flowers. They came to look at our new delivery table, and at the autoclave—nobody in these parts had ever seen such a shiny gizmo for sterilizing things."

"I imagine it was quite a relief for you and Susie not to have to deliver babies in the hills any more," I said.

"We still had to go out there some," she said. "But it was a relief not to have to go so often."

5

On my most recent visit to Morehead I noticed that the little sign that said "C. Louise Caudill, M.D." had disappeared from the lawn in front of the one-story brick clinic on Main Street. Though the clinic remains in operation, Louise no longer wants to draw attention to that fact; at seventy-five, she is trying to "cut down" on her practice, which means, I would guess, treating no more patients than a family doctor normally would. (She stopped her practice in obstetrics in December 1981.) When I entered the building, Louise was in the examining room with a patient; two or three others were in the waiting room, reading magazines. What a difference from the line of people I remembered waiting on every step of the staircase nearly four decades earlier!

During an earlier stay in Morehead, Jean and I questioned Louise and Susie one night about the patients they had seen that day. Louise guessed they had treated about thirty people at the clinic, many of them children —some of them for preschool physicals, some brought in without an appointment by a parent because of a special problem or emergency. "Things just come on that we handle between appointments," Susie said. "We had a little kid with fever and vomiting, and another with earache. And a woman came in who had a sudden allergic response to something or other; she said she had been sweeping up some sand."

"And then there was that little girl with something more peculiar," Louise said. "A Japanese beetle crawled into her ear, and just didn't want to come out."

"You might have coaxed it out with a mating call, or maybe the kind of scent they put in beetle traps," I said.

"This little beetle was *daid,*" Louise said. "It had got

all squished up, way back in the ear, from somebody's finger trying to get it out. It took some doing, to get at it."

The advent of St. Claire Medical Center brought dozens of doctors to the region, general practitioners and specialists alike, and so (largely through Louise's own efforts in establishing the hospital) her patient load had declined to more manageable proportions long before she took down her sign. But for the first six years of the clinic's operation it must have been difficult to avoid chaos in its rooms, for babies were being born there while all the other patients were waiting their turn to see the doctor and nurse. A picture from this period that appeared in a later issue of the Morehead *News* (the twice-weekly successor of W. E. Crutcher's weekly Rowan County *News*) shows Louise and Susie in the clinic, smiling at each other; each of them is holding a set of twins.

But four babies born at almost the same time did not constitute a record at their little clinic; the record was set, as if by Divine Providence, on the day that Monsignor Charles Towell, director of hospitals for the Covington, Kentucky, diocese, arrived to investigate whether or not Morehead really needed a hospital. "Babies and mothers were everywhere when he came in the door," Louise remembers, for five babies—"two sets of twins and a single"—had been born that day.

"We didn't have near enough bassinets," Susie said,

"so we just lined the babies up on that couch in the waiting room."

Instrumental as she was to be in bringing a hospital to town, Louise admits to being initially opposed to one in Morehead. "For a long time, people were saying we needed a hospital," she said. "*Everybody* wanted a hospital, but I was against it. I'd seen so many bad things done in little hospitals, places that were just for putting patients in beds. In little hospitals in the small towns, a surgeon can be knife-happy, and nobody to stop him or offer the patient another opinion."

"What changed your mind?" I asked.

"Well, there was a man who came through town, a doctor—Dr. Howard was his name—and he worked for the state in public health. Nobody had invited him to my knowledge; he just came into my office one day, looked at our whole setup, and said, 'You can have a hospital in this town if you want one.' "

"Was he suggesting you could get money for it from the state?"

"Oh, no, not at all. He just said there was no reason for us not having a hospital. I told him I didn't want a hospital unless it was going to be a good one, and he asked me what my idea of a good hospital would be. I said we needed three things to have a good hospital: enough money for a decent building and the proper equipment; somebody to run it right, an experienced administrator who could get the trained nurses and so on; and credibility—that is, a good medical staff, people who know their stuff, surgeons and other specialists, radiologists, pathologists."

"And what did Dr. Howard say to that?"

"He just said, 'You can have all that, if you want it.' "

"But he never told you how to go about getting it?"

"No. As I say, he just was coming through town and told me that, and after he was gone, I sat there and thought, he thinks we can do it, and by granny! I think he's right."

Neither Louise nor Susie knows much more about Dr. Howard than that, though Susie, with her better recall of such details, said his initials were C. C. "Dr. C. C. Howard of Glasgow," she said, remembering the town he came from at the moment she gave his full name. (Glasgow is a town in south-central Kentucky, not far from Mammoth Cave.) "I think he used to have a practice there."

"Did he ever come back?" I asked.

"We never saw him again," Susie said.

Unlike the man from Porlock whose knock on Coleridge's door not only interrupted the poet's transcription of a poem about Xanadu that had come to him in a dream, but shattered his memory of it, causing the poem to remain the fragment that has come down to us, Louise's visitor from Glasgow managed, with his few words of optimism, to build a dream in her own mind far grander than her earlier dream of a clinic.

"And he *was* right, of course," Louise said. "Three years later—even less than that, more like two and a half—we had just the kind of hospital he told us we could have. Now that's something of a miracle, don't you reckon?"

Louise, who is on the board of directors of St. Claire Medical Center, arranged for Jean and me to be taken on a tour of its facilities. It has undergone considerable expansion since it opened for its initial patient in 1963; having just learned of its existence, it certainly seemed like a miracle to me. We were given a demonstration of the machine that through sound waves can construct an image of what lies within a patient's body, and looked at the machine that makes CAT scans; we saw all the other modern radiology equipment. The hospital was as advanced as the new hospital in my own prosperous and populous upstate New York county, and the patient rooms were larger, more inviting. I was bewildered by the bright lights, the shining floors, the nurses in their nuns' habits walking briskly on their errands, the loudspeakers calling for one doctor or another to report to this or that clinic or floor—all of this going on in a town that never conceivably could have supported such a facility in my days of living there, and which despite its recent growth still seemed much too small, with its 170 beds, St. Claire Medical Center belonged, I thought, in a metropolitan setting.

I asked our guide where all the patients came from. He said the hospital's service area covers eleven northeastern counties with a total population of 150,000. In addition to the patients who come to the major facility in Morehead, about 40,000 each year visit the hospital's primary care clinics in Rowan and three other counties —Bath, Menifee, and Carter. These clinics are staffed by family physicians, nurse practitioners, and certified midwives. And he said that the hospital also administers a home health program that now makes nearly 30,000 patient visitations a year.

In walking through its corridors with a guide, I did think of Coleridge's poem, and the differing consequences of the visits made by the strangers from Porlock and Glasgow; for the hospital seemed magical enough to belong in Xanadu, a place as remote as Rowan County once had seemed to me. In the years that the paucity of doctors and lack of facilities had put the most severe demands on them, Louise and Susie sometimes had traveled even beyond the borders of their own county. They had gone into the hamlets and countryside of Bath and Carter counties to deliver babies and to administer to those who were severely ill. With its network of clinics and home services, St. Claire Medical Center was serving a goal that had been so crucial to the doctor and nurse—that of helping rural people—and to a degree that the pair of them, whatever their dedication, never had been able to achieve.

That evening, having dinner with Louise and Susie at their home, I said to Louise that Dr. C. C. Howard certainly had put a great idea into her head, but that I couldn't imagine how everything had come to pass the way he had foretold.

"He made me believe," she said. "Sometimes all it takes is the believing and then everything snaps into place."

It is true enough that in a surprisingly short time after Dr. Howard spoke to Louise, the hospital—then with but forty-one beds—opened for its first patient; but it required both good fortune and much perseverance on her part before things could "snap into place." The people of Rowan County obviously wanted a hospital as much as they once wanted to learn how to read and write; but to achieve the *kind* of hospital that Louise desired was a much more intricate task than Cora Wilson Stewart's campaign to eradicate illiteracy from the county. What Louise had in mind required far more money, and the support of other institutions. Her task was similar to Cora Wilson Stewart's, though, in its dependence upon others possessing a similar optimism, a similar idealism. The earlier woman depended upon the schoolteachers in the county; Louise upon local community leaders, a Catholic order, and professionals in her own field at the newly opened Medical Center of the University of Kentucky in Lexington. The support of the first group led to that of the second; but only with the assistance of the third could "everything snap into place." Solving a puzzle with three such interlinking parts, some of which didn't initially want to fit, was an activity that probably gave Louise more "fun" than anything she has ever undertaken. Certainly she smiles, and her eyes take on that humorous glint she is famous for, when she talks about fitting the pieces together.

6

Susie remembers that Dr. Howard passed through Morehead in August 1960. (Recently, I received a letter from a doctor who had known him at roughly this period and who remembers him as "an influential physician . . . a wonderful man with a great foresight," words borne out, certainly, by what was to happen in Morehead.) According to Louise, it was only a few days after Dr. Howard's visit that she and Susie began "going around from house to house in town, to all the people who had the most money" to see if there would be sufficient financial support for the kind of hospital that she envisioned. (Other people then were also meeting to talk about securing a hospital, but Louise and Susie at the time didn't try to contact them, for none of them had in mind anything more than an unaccredited "lying-in" facility.)

Their canvass sufficiently encouraged Louise to call a meeting at her office in order to "get this thing going." For this initial meeting, held before the month was up, she selected people "like Adron Doran [the president of the college], J. M. ('Chin') Clayton [a local businessman who ran the Eagles' Nest restaurant], and Glenn Lane [cashier and one of the directors of the Citizens Bank of Morehead, the major competitor of the Caudill family's Peoples Bank of Morehead]"—the kind of people, Louise said, "who would have influence on other people."

Louise worked rapidly toward the establishment of the kind of hospital she, and now the people who had met with her, wanted. Of her three requirements for a good hospital, the easiest to accomplish, she says, was "getting the money." She and Susie, after all, had already contacted those residents (they remain anonymous) who would be the most generous individual benefactors, and knew the extent of their promised gifts. And already W. E. Crutcher had been using the pages of his Rowan County *News* to publicize the need for a local hospital. (Besides being concerned about the well-being of the community, he knew, from personal experience, about the difficulties in getting proper medical care in emergencies: his wife was seriously ill, requiring treatment elsewhere; she was to die before the hospital opened.) On the day—November 27, 1960—that the fund drive commenced with a dinner, the Rowan County *News* issued a four-page supplement about the proposed hospital that requested communitywide generosity in raising the quarter million dollars needed from local residents.

Through President Doran, the college became as important to the success of the fund drive as the newspaper. Before assuming the presidency in 1954, Doran had been a Church of Christ minister as well as an educator, basketball coach, and politician. Though he had been in office only two years when I left Morehead State College for Cornell, I knew something about Doran's ability to get things done. Shortly after he became president, I was awakened one dawn by the sound of what seemed a battalion of tanks invading town. Doran, having heard that the college band, in practicing on the football field in rainy weather, often turned the grass surface into mud, had managed, through his political influence, to divert much of the heavy highway equipment in eastern Kentucky to Morehead, in order to level a small hill to make a practice field for the exclusive use of the band.

In the years following my departure, the college under his guidance prospered as it never had before; and apparently he became accustomed to having matters proceed according to his dictation. He was to become locally famous—or infamous—for one particular act of autocracy, years after I had left. Vexed by the decision of the Morehead City Council to draw municipal water from an inexhaustible new source about ten miles from town (Cave Run Lake, created by a huge dam constructed by the Army Corps of Engineers on the Licking River) instead of continuing to buy water supplied by the college from its lake, Doran shut off the water to all the town's faucets for one memorable day.

Louise and most of the other townspeople, though, applauded the means he used to secure generous dona-

175

tions to the fund drive from everybody on the college faculty and staff. As I heard from a number of people in town, he called a special meeting of the employees. "Ladies and gentlemen," he is reported to have said during his brief address, "I am donating five percent of my annual salary to the hospital fund, and I expect you to do the same."

An expert from Boston was called in to direct the fund drive, but Louise and Susie did much of the leg-work, knocking on the doors of citizens they hadn't previously contacted. By the end of December, the campaign had exceeded its goal, and by a generous margin. (Forty percent of the amount came from college employees.)

While it is a considerable sum for the citizens of a small town to contribute—Morehead had 3,100 inhabitants in 1956, and probably no more than 4,000 in 1960 —the $294,000 pledged during the drive wasn't enough to build a good hospital even in those days; the estimated amount, which turned out to be several hundred thousand dollars too low, was $850,000.

Actually, Louise knew that if the campaign were successful, the chances were good that not only the remainder of the money would be forthcoming from two additional sources, but that the second of her three requirements, an experienced administrative and nursing staff, would be met as well. In the days following the meeting she had held at her office with President Doran and others, she tried to get Baptist and Methodist support for the hospital, knowing that both churches operated hospitals throughout the country. When these attempts failed, she turned to Monsignor Towell of the Covington diocese of the Catholic church, who happened to be a member of the Kentucky Hill-Burton hospital committee and hence one who could be of service in securing not only Catholic support in financing and operating the hospital, but federal assistance through the funds made available by the Hill-Burton legislation passed by Congress.

Given his influence, Monsignor Towell seems the obvious person for Louise to have contacted at the beginning; but given the religious disposition of the area, I can see the reason that she would turn to the Catholics only as an apparent last resort.

If Cora Wilson Stewart's crusade against illiteracy brought to mind some passages in Agee's *Let Us Now Praise Famous Men,* Louise's attempt to establish a hospital, complicated as it was by religious issues, caused me to return to a book that has been compared to Agee's. Harry M. Caudill's *Night Comes to the Cumberlands* is the most impassioned and eloquent book about the social and economic sufferings of eastern Kentucky that I know of. A journalist and former member of the Kentucky House of Representatives from Whitesburg (in Letcher County, near the West Virginia border), Caudill, who died in 1991, probably was related to Louise (whose grandfather, after all, had come from Letcher County), though I don't think they ever met.

While *Night Comes to the Cumberlands* emphasizes the despoliation of human and natural resources that accompanied the mining of coal, a ravage that spared Rowan County, he writes also of the history and general culture of the mountainous Cumberland plateau that includes Rowan. "For many years and indeed, to this day," he writes, in a passage describing the dominant religious attitudes of the area,

there were "hard-shell" preachers, so named because their doctrine was so harsh. They preached, among other things, the cruel doctrine of infant damnation. To their fanatical minds it was apparent that if a man could not enter the kingdom of heaven until he had been spiritually "born again," even a little child was shut out of the Celestial Kingdom if death came prior to an age when awareness of sin had brought repentance and rebirth. And it followed that if failure to be born again excluded the soul from heaven, that soul must certainly go to hell. This fantastic nonsense anguished generations of mountain parents, nearly all of whom had seen more than one infant die.

The wellspring of these folk churches was a stern Calvinism which the Scotch element of the population had carried with it from the dour highlands. Without competition from other religious ideas or doctrines it slowly pervaded the whole populace, and eventually became deeply rooted in their mores, so widely and unquestionably accepted as to constitute unwritten law. And while its adherents might split into a myriad of disputing minor sects, they were to remain steadfastly loyal to its basic tenets. One of these was a hatred for the Roman Catholic Church and the Pope as nothing less than arms of Satan. Another was confession of sins "before men," and a third was the requirement of baptism. Still another was an immutable principle that no preacher or minister be compensated in any way for his time or work. Their Biblical hero was John the Baptist, and each church was fiercely proud to call itself "Baptist," the members insisting that they alone were true followers of the methods and doctrines of the prophet. Each group, also, claimed to trace its origins back through the ages to this forerunner of Christ. This curious idea, now a folk notion throughout the region, resulted in the use of such church names as "Regular," "Old Regular," "Bed-Rock," and "Primitive" Baptists. These groups in subsequent years were to split again and again, like endlessly dividing amoebae, in fierce wrangles over the very meaning of the word "baptism."

Such divisions were still going on in Morehead during the years my family lived there; so many permutations occurred that sometimes it was difficult for an outsider to discover the original sect. A radical group split off from its more conservative parent to build a small brick church just opposite the juncture of our little dead-end street, Caudill Court, with Main Street; from our open windows in summertime, we could hear the preacher of the evening moving from conventional speech into an unknown tongue, and the waves of emotion his sounds induced in the congregation. (One of

that church's preachers gifted in unknown tongues—
for there were several of them—earned his living as a
mechanic for Bob Day's Oldsmobile agency.) I learned
that another sect in town secretly used poisonous snakes
in its rituals, though such use had been made illegal by
state legislation.

I first read *Night Comes to the Cumberlands* in my early
years at Cornell (it was published in 1962), and was
surprised to discover how small a percentage of the
rural people belonged to any church: "Not more than
12 to 15 percent now have church membership or affiliation," Caudill writes, "though countless dedicated
evangelists have worn themselves out in proselytizing
labors. Today the plateau probably contains the lowest
percentage of actual church membership to be found in
any other region of Christendom."

That small percentage, though, carried a potent
force. The few Catholics in the region kept a low pro-
file. There was no Catholic church in Morehead when
Susie first came to town in 1948. She told me she
doubted she would have come, whatever her friendship
with Louise, had not a priest traveled to the town every
Sunday to celebrate Mass. Catholics were considered
such an exotic species even by educated people, Susie
said, laughing as she remembered it, that Louise's own
mother never could remember whether Susie was Catholic or Jewish.

"Where did you hold Mass?" I asked.

"In a garage behind somebody's house," she said.

"A two- or three-stall garage?"

"No, just one stall," she said. "There was plenty of room, though."

For me, Harry M. Caudill's description of religion in the Cumberlands gives drama to an open meeting held on October 7 (soon after Louise had met with President Doran and others to plan their opening strategy) at the Rowan County Health Center and attended by about seventy-five people interested in obtaining a local hospital. They included business and professional leaders, municipal and county officials, and clergymen. The only written account of that meeting I've seen is in an unpublished paper written in May 1968 by a student in a graduate history course at Morehead State College. I was given a copy of it by the present administrator of St. Claire Medical Center, Sister Mary Jeannette, who warned me that she'd been told it contained some serious factual errors. Still, the following sentences, based on the minutes of the organization (the Northeast Kentucky Hospital Foundation) formed at that meeting, are probably accurate enough:

> After some time Dr. Caudill arrived in the company of a Catholic priest, Monsignor Charles Towell, who she introduced as a priest of the Catholic diocese of Covington, Kentucky. . . . As a first order of business Dr. Caudill asked if the citizens assembled wished to start a hospital association in Morehead which could act as a non-profit agency to raise money locally, apply for federal funds, and make other necessary arrangements to get

Morehead a hospital. The proposal was overwhelmingly approved. Dr. Caudill was elected chairman of the organization just formed and given power to appoint a temporary planning committee. Msgr. Towell then spoke saying that Hill-Burton funds for one-third of the cost of construction of the hospital would almost certainly be available and probably funds for one-half. Also he felt sure he could find some Catholic sisters to operate the hospital. However, he had no intention of cooperating if any serious religious prejudice was evidenced.

7

In speaking with Louise about that meeting, I read those words about it to her, emphasizing the final sentence. "Yes, the subject of religion did come up," she said, but she dismissed it with a wave of her hand. The hostility toward Catholicism that might have prevented the successful establishment of a hospital run by a Catholic order apparently never was of major concern to her— no more consequential than the earlier possibility of sexual discrimination against her as the first woman to practice medicine in the county. (She dismisses as equally trivial or beneath consideration the question of small-town bias toward her for never marrying and raising a family of her own. When one journalist or another attempts to pry into her personal life, wondering why this woman who loves children and has delivered so many babies never wanted to be a mother herself, she simply responds, as an article about her in the January 26, 1979, Morehead *News* reports, "that it was so late when she started medical school that she had neither the time nor the inclination for a family of her own.")

But I suspect she has triumphed over convention and prejudice, not so much from a refusal to admit to their existence, as from the effect her presence—the glow of a woman "following her bliss"—had on others. Judge Elijah Hogge was one of the executive committee members of the Northeastern Kentucky Hospital Foundation created at that October 7, 1960, meeting at the Rowan County Health Center; he served both as its treasurer and attorney, drawing up all the legal documents. He told me that the people who came to the open meeting did so not only because they saw the need for a hospital, but because Louise "had so much interest in it; they wanted to help her and at the same time help themselves. She sparkled when she talked about it," and they felt good to be "doing something for Louise. So we started raising money and she got a commitment from the Sisters of Notre Dame that they would participate and operate the hospital."

Unlike Louise, Lige remembers the local prejudice to Catholics as anything but trivial; resistance came not only from "primitive" or "hard-shell" Baptists but from many other members of the community. Catholic involvement was a "touchy" issue for the whole town, even though "everybody wanted the hospital in the worst way." Even those who gave to the fund drive had to overcome their reluctance "to give to the Catholic order." And he said that "they preached venom from the pulpits" of certain churches for a time. That kind of opposition "just had to be squelched, for we could see that it would kill the whole deal."

Though officials of the Baptist and Methodist churches had already refused Louise financial or other assistance, she and Lige and other members of the executive committee encouraged all who were hostile toward Catholic participation to persuade the state and national headquarters of any Protestant denomination of their choice to support and operate the proposed hospital. "That offer kind of squelched the opposition," he said, for everybody soon realized that no other church was willing to meet "the gigantic problems we would have in creating a hospital here, and keeping it in operation."

One supplementary benefit of having a modern medical center in Morehead, Lige said, came from the arrival of the Catholic order in town. Meeting and getting to know the nuns became "part of our educative process;" the whole town learned how "bigoted and backward we had been." Norma, Lige's wife, who had been listening to my conversation with him, agreed with that remark. "Yes, so many people had been worried about the area being destroyed by Catholics. But the sisters of Notre Dame were so dedicated! They lived on the top floor of the hospital, and there was no air conditioning then; they served people who were dying, staying up with them all night long. Their children would tell other people, 'A sister stayed with my mother,' and pretty soon the hostility was gone, and everybody was grateful."

Lige didn't know what had persuaded the Covington Catholic diocese to come to Morehead's assistance. "It must have been their heed to Dr. Louise's plea with them, and their reasoning that the area did need help," he said. "And I think Louise reached them at an opportune moment, for the Sisters of Notre Dame had just closed a hospital deeper in the mountains and so had a trained staff available—administrators, people to look after the books, to run the kitchen, to take care of the patients, and so on." (That hospital was in Jenkins, not far from Harry M. Caudill's Whitesburg, and its apparently unavoidable closing another blow to that depressed mining region.)

W. E. Crutcher, chairman of the publicity committee of the Northeast Kentucky Hospital Foundation, ran major stories on the groundbreaking ceremony in each of the three issues of the Rowan County *News* preceding that event. If the final story carried the streamer "Greatest Day Since College Established" above the headline, in the penultimate issue the streamer read "The Day We Have Been Praying For." The article in that issue begins, "Ground breaking for Morehead's new hospital—Saint Claire—will be at the site [a natural enough assumption], intersection of 2nd Street and

Fleming Avenue, the afternoon of Friday, Sept. 29
[1961]," and continues,

Announcement of the long awaited start of construction
. . . was made this morning following a meeting of the
14 member steering committee composed of Northeast
Kentucky Hospital Foundation, Inc., and Monsignor
Charles A. Towell, Covington Diocesan Director of
Catholic Hospitals. . . .

First spade of dirt will be turned by Most Reverend
Richard E. Ackerman, Bishop of the Diocese of Coving-
ton. The principal address will come from Dr. Adron
Doran, President of Morehead State College.

Commonwealth Attorney Elijah M. Hogge will be
Master of Ceremonies. Also on the program are Rev.
John Conley, pastor of the First Church of God, who
will give the invocation; Rev. Thomas Ditto, pastor of
the Morehead Methodist Church, who will render the
benediction and Hospital Foundation President C. P.
Caudill [Louise's uncle and president of the Peoples
Bank] who will present [the] Sisters of Notre Dame, who
will operate the hospital; members of the steering committee; and Dr. C. Louise Caudill for whom the hospital,
in a sense, was named.

The ceremony starts at 2 o'clock on the 29th with a
downtown parade by the Rowan County High School.
The band of Morehead State College will furnish music
at the site, and is scheduled for one number during the
ceremonies.

Caudill said that Major William H. Layne and County
Judge Carl Jones will issue a proclamation asking all busi-

ness places to close for two hours—from 2 P.M. until 4
P.M.—on the day of ground breaking. . . .

Though Crutcher didn't sell the newspaper until
1976, he must have turned over much of the reportorial
work to others at the time the name was changed to the
Morehead *News* in 1962 or 1963, for the writing style
becomes less flamboyant. The paper gave wide, but
more restrained, coverage to the June 1963 dedication
of the hospital.

Baptist clergymen of even the more liberal sects seem
to have been absent from this ceremony, as they were
from the one for the groundbreaking, for they are not
mentioned in the news accounts of either event. Prayers
were offered by Bishop Ackerman, as well as by two
local Protestant pastors—Reverend Conley of the First
Church of God, joined this time by Reverend Charles
L. Brooks, pastor of Louise's own Christian church.
The major address was by Dr. William R. Willard, vice
president and dean of the recently established University of Kentucky Medical Center. Monsignor Towell,
who laid the cornerstone, gave a shorter speech. In it,
he acknowledged the effectiveness of Louise's letters
and phone calls, which finally brought him to Morehead on an investigatory trip, and he described the effect
on him as he stepped into her clinic, filled as it was that
day with mothers and their newborn babies. The Morehead *News* journalist, while making more deletions
from Towell's speech than Crutcher probably would

have, gives the essence of his remarks. Referring "to the
call [that had] come from Dr. Caudill," he said that

> . . . it was a pathetic plea for her people. . . . We have
> many such requests . . . but she would not give up and
> she called and called and pleaded and pleaded. . . . So I
> decided to come to Morehead. . . . When I arrived at her
> offices I saw four newborn babies [had the fifth still been
> in the delivery room, I wonder?], and they all seemed to
> be reaching out for help. . . . Then and there I decided if
> possible, under God, I would do something for this com-
> munity.

The article goes on to remark that "the crowd
applauded" his remarks, and "kept applauding when
Dr. Caudill was introduced. She made a brief, simple
speech" in which she referred to the medical center as a
symbol of the united nature of the community and the
diverse faiths that had made it possible.

In the major address, Dr. Willard told the audience,

> "The eyes of the medical profession in Kentucky . . .
> yes, in the United States . . . are looking on you today,
> and your future planning and progress will be closely
> observed."

Dr. Willard was referring to the almost-without-
precedent manner in which St. Claire Medical Center
will be conducted.

Sisters of Notre Dame own and administer the hospital. But, in order to attract doctors and specialists to
Morehead, a "Professional Fund" was created, and a
cooperative arrangement finalized with the UK center.

(It is believed no other hospital in the nation has such a three-prong agreement.)

If by "the eyes of the medical profession," Dr. Willard was referring to the American Medical Association—particularly its state affiliate, the Kentucky Medical Association—or such other groups as the Kentucky Academy of General Practice, he surely was correct in assuming they were watching closely. With the encouragement of Dr. Willard and the advice and support of two idealists on the University of Kentucky Medical Center staff, Louise had embraced a structure for meeting her third requirement—a staff of skilled specialists. The structure, being innovative, was bound to arouse the antagonism of entrenched professional organizations.

8

Dr. Willard and the two other doctors from the University of Kentucky Medical Center who gave particular assistance to Louise in bringing her "good" hospital into existence have long since left the state. One of them, Dr. Richard Segnitz, a pediatrics surgeon for more than thirty years, is now "a rural doctor, much like Louise," he told me in a telephone conversation from his cabin above the Missouri Breaks in Montana. He is employed by the Public Health Service and has an office in a hospital adjacent to a reservation; many of his patients are Indians. The other, Dr. Edmund D. Pellegrino, who then was professor and chairman of the department of medicine at the center, is now director of the Kennedy Institute of Ethics and John Carroll Professor of Medicine and Medical Humanities at Georgetown University in Washington, D.C.

Of the two, Segnitz gave the greater personal help, often driving from Lexington to Morehead to confer with Louise about problems and their solutions, to suggest organizations that might offer financial support for a hospital, to recommend the names of physicians for the hospital staff, and so on. Most of the actual grant applications were the work of Robert Johnson, Willard's administrative assistant, another strong supporter of the proposed Morehead hospital. "Dick Segnitz came up a million times," Louise told me. But it was Pellegrino, who also made a number of visits, who suggested the kind of structure that, despite the hostility of the medical associations, enabled St. Claire Medical Center in its crucial beginning years to attract specialists with an unusually strong commitment to patient care— that is, doctors not unlike Louise herself.

Louise first met Segnitz in Lexington in 1961, at a symposium on heart problems. Open-heart surgery was a new technique at the time, and Segnitz, a member of the team that had performed the first such operation in Kentucky, spoke on the topic. The story of their meeting is one Louise likes to tell. Before the symposium, and during the intermissions, she talked with him about her hopes for the Morehead hospital. At one point, she told him that she "wanted to find somebody to get us going," and he replied, as she remembers it, " 'I think I know such a person.' " After the symposium ended, Louise says that "she tagged along after him," wanting to find out the name of the individual he had in mind. "I asked him, 'Who? Who is this person?' 'To tell the truth,' he admitted [and here Louise, in retelling this old story to me, chuckled], 'I was thinking about myself.' "

Indeed, he not only agreed to be on the staff of the new hospital, but indicated his willingness to serve as its initial director. He was intrigued by the possibilities of a plan suggested by Pellegrino, who had helped to institute a similar one at a new hospital in New Jersey. At Pellegrino's suggestion, Segnitz, Louise, Susie, and Sister Mary Edwin (appointed as the first administrator of St. Claire) traveled to Flemington, New Jersey, to visit that hospital, the Hunterdon County Medical Center, which had been in operation for almost a decade. Before coming to Kentucky to help establish its new center, Pellegrino—much of whose professional life has been devoted, as he says, "to starting things from scratch"—was medical director and chairman of the department of medicine of the Hunterdon center, and he thought that its philosophy and organizational structure, which he felt to be in keeping with attitudes about medicine he shared with Louise, Segnitz, and Sister

Mary Edwin, could serve as a model for the new hospital in Morehead.

A book-length "interim report" on the Hunterdon center, written by its first director, Dr. Ray E. Trussell, was published in 1955 by Harvard University Press under the title *Hunterdon Medical Center: The Story of One Approach to Rural Medical Care*. In his acknowledgments, Trussell expresses gratitude to Pellegrino, "the present director of the Center, who worked so effectively to get the Center under way and still serves as director of internal medicine." (Pellegrino, who had come to Hunterdon as chief of medicine in 1953, left in 1959 for the new challenge at Lexington.)

What Louise found at Hunterdon delighted her. Two women—Mrs. Rose Z. Angell, the county welfare director, and Mrs. William F. Leicester, a local resident with experience in organization and public relations—had been as instrumental as Louise in getting a campaign for a hospital under way and, again like Louise, had held out for a hospital that was more than a conventional "lying-in" facility. Hunterdon had been fortunate in developing a unique relationship with Bellevue Hospital in New York that, as Trussell describes it,

> would not only provide to the local physicians an opportunity for professional development but would also bring to the people of a rural county medical and health services of the highest quality. By this alliance the rural center would, in turn, develop into a teaching unit, not only for practicing physicians, but also for medical students,

interns and residents, nurses, and those in the so-called paramedical occupations and professions.

Probably the most unusual feature of the Hunterdon Medical Center . . . is the appointment of general practitioners of the county to the staff of the hospital. Under this type of staff organization they assume the responsibilities of medical care of the local citizens jointly with the full-time specialists who direct the various departments of the center. No record of a previous experimental organization of this kind has been found in the annals of American medicine.

While Trussell's book provides a clear exposition of the beginnings and philosophy of the Hunterdon center, which indeed became the model for the Morehead hospital, I felt it would be helpful to talk with Pellegrino, who had been so influential in the Morehead decision. Besides, the entries about him in *Who's Who in America* and the various volumes devoted to medical biographies intrigued me, for he obviously has played an important role in a number of administrative and structural innovations that have come to American medicine.

After helping to develop the University of Kentucky Medical Center, Pellegrino became dean of the new School of Medicine at the State University of New York at Stony Brook and founding director of the Health Sciences Center there. The center includes, in addition to the medical school, others in dentistry, nursing, allied health, and social welfare—the largest comprehensive health sciences center "started from scratch" in the United States and perhaps in the world. He left Stony Brook in 1973 to become chancellor of the Center for the Health Sciences, vice president for health affairs, and professor of medicine and humanities in medicine at the University of Tennessee at Memphis, managing, in his two-year tenure, to institute a statewide program of clinical campuses linked with the one at Memphis. Then he went to Yale as president and chairman of the Yale–New Haven Medical Center, his task there to devise a new administrative structure while serving also as a professor of medicine.

In 1978, Pellegrino was appointed president of the Catholic University of America in Washington, D.C., and a professor of philosophy and biology, somehow also finding time to be a professor of clinical medicine and community medicine at Georgetown University School of Medicine. He became a professor of medicine and medical humanities at Georgetown in 1982, and the following year the director of that university's Kennedy Institute of Ethics, a "think tank" on ethical issues involving law, business, technology, international relations, and applied ethics, as well as medicine and biology. He remains in both those posts at Georgetown.

Pellegrino has accomplished so much in his lifetime that I wondered, in taking a taxi to the Kennedy Institute in October 1988, if he would remember much about a smallish hospital in Rowan County that he once had been interested in, and about a rural doctor there. It turned out that he remembers his Kentucky years with remarkable clarity. Talking about humanistic ideals brings a shine to his eyes (reminding me of the gleam in Louise's) and even makes his nose wiggle, when he expresses a strong feeling, but he arranges his thoughts in a concise and logical progression. He is a slender man of average height, in his late sixties.

"Louise," Pellegrino said, "had the same kind of dedication to quality that I had encountered in the women of Hunterdon County. Her motivations were the highest; her part absolutely essential." An outsider can't come in with a plan, he explained; there must be "somebody on the inside who says 'this is a good plan . . . '" Louise bought the idea completely."

The Hunterdon plan that she "bought" had been developed in a rural New Jersey area with no hospital and no medical specialists. ("Yes, there is a rural New Jersey, too," Pellegrino said, remarking that, at least in post–World War II, the main income for Hunterdon County's 65,000 residents came from dairy and poultry operations.) Pellegrino acknowledged that he had a major role in the Hunterdon philosophy, though, he said, "it would be unfair to say it was mine." The original concept of affiliation with a university, and of a hospital with full-time chiefs of service who also would serve on the faculty of that university, had already been sketched out by a consultant from the New York Academy of Medicine, Dr. E. H. L. Corwin. Pellegrino had been brought in "to help fill in what all this meant."

Pellegrino essentially set up the program. "You can imagine," he said, "what this means to a thirty-two-year-old guy—to come out to a rural community and say what we're going to do!" He enumerated for me the chief features of the planned new program, beginning with its enhancement of the role of county practitioners.

First, "every practitioner in the county would have de facto hospital privileges in medicine" and "would have a choice: to care for the patient himself under the supervision of the chief of medicine, or to ask for formal consultation." In the former case, the practitioner would "write the orders and arrange for the discharge of the patient, and so on," although Pellegrino would "make rounds every day, seeing the patients with the house staff and medical students." The practitioner could have an informal consultation with Pellegrino "any time he wanted it without cost to the patient." Under the other option the patient would be turned over to Pellegrino for continuing or temporary care. Intended to keep a balance between full-time specialists and practitioners, this system "worked splendidly in the seven years I was there," Pellegrino said. "It was something we haven't achieved in many places: it remains an ideal, and I'm enthusiastic about it still."

Second, "it would be a teaching hospital, with doctors teaching doctors" in accordance with the method worked out by the New York University–Bellevue Medical Center staff. Third, the plan would provide

comprehensive care, ranging from " preventive to ter-
tiary to primary [care], from curative physical ailments
to social work, and so on."

A final feature—"talk about revolutionary principles!" Pellegrino exclaimed, his nose giving a little
twitch—was that "full-time members of the hospital
staff would be salaried, thus not in competition with the
practitioners." Since they received a salary, the specialists would have "no financial incentive to do things not
required." There would be no unnecessary surgery. "It
was two years before our surgery department took out
a normal appendix!" he declared, with a smile. Pediatrician, psychiatrist, surgeon—all were to be paid the
same amount.

In discussing with me her attitudes toward medicine,
Louise had referred several times to the Hunterdon plan
as one that suited her philosophy; it must have seemed
to her a confirmation of her own views when, in visit-
ing the Hunterdon center, she perceived the apparently
successful operation of such a plan. She liked, of course,
the emphasis on the county practitioner, the one who
all along had treated the patient, and who in the Hunterdon scheme not only was the one who saw to it that
the patient was admitted to the hospital, but could continue taking care of the patient after admission. Beyond
this, Louise approved of the salary arrangement. "To
my mind, that's the right idea," she said. "You ought
to be equally equal. Here's something that's always
bothered me: the surgeon comes in and makes, say, two

cuts, and then sews everything up. He makes all the money; the guy who does the workout, who had diagnosed the problem, who tells the surgeon what to do, gets much less." (In recent years, though, she admits to having changed her ideas a little: "Some of those surgeons," she confessed to me, "are pretty darn smart.")

Like Louise, the Sisters of Notre Dame approved of the concept, once it had been explained to them; Pellegrino said he found it much harder "to sell his plan to the church officials." With the sisters who were planning the hospital, he made separate visits to Bishop Ackerman and Monsignor Towell. The latter became skeptical of Pellegrino's enthusiasm for a Hunterdon-type plan at Morehead. Pellegrino remembers Towell as saying, "Before you get into all of this, tell me, if you were so successful at Hunterdon, why did you come down to Kentucky?" The implication of that remark, Pellegrino told me, "was that anybody who came to Kentucky couldn't be worth much," and he responded to it carefully and as honestly as he could: "I said, 'With all respect, Monsignor, you must appreciate that I regard the ideas being developed at the University of Kentucky Medical Center and the possibilities at Morehead to be challenges of the greatest significance to me personally and to American medicine. I've always based my decisions on a job on the pursuit of an ideal, and here in Kentucky I'm in pursuit of the same ideal—how to improve rural health care—that I was in New Jersey.' "

Pellegrino said that he had been distressed upon coming to Kentucky "by the feeling that somehow the people from the Northeast were smarter. That kind of inferiority is preposterous; it produces defensiveness, sometimes bravado. The Medical School at the University of Kentucky was a pioneer at the time in a whole series of things," including rural health and the establishment of satellite teaching hospitals. (The hope had been for a series of them, but St. Claire remains the only such satellite in the state.) "Yale, Harvard, Columbia weren't doing anything extraordinary at the time," Pellegrino told me. "Kentucky was, and that's why I went there."

Louise, that unusually modest doctor, says that her success in bringing to Morehead the kind of hospital that met, or perhaps even surpassed, her own concept of a "good" one was wholly a matter of fortunate timing. That is, Dr. Howard brought her the belief in its possibility at the right moment; Monsignor Towell arrived at her clinic when it was filled with more than enough babies to astonish him; and she met Segnitz, Willard, and Pellegrino just as they were looking for a way to achieve something new that would be extraordinary.

9

Excavation for the hospital already had been completed by the time the Northeast Kentucky Medical Foundation, with Monsignor Towell's consent, reached an arrangement with the University of Kentucky Medical Center to make St. Claire a teaching hospital based largely on the Hunterdon plan. Partly because the hospital would be owned by the Sisters of Notre Dame, whereas the specialists would be salaried employees of the local foundation, an addition to the hospital, providing offices and clinical space for these specialists, was necessary at once; these were the changes in the architectural plans that made mandatory the supplementary fund drive. In its issue of February 15, 1962, the Rowan County *News* revealed the story of the "new development" that "almost from a clear sky" had resolved the staffing problem of the yet-to-be constructed hospital, ensuring its status as "a major health facility instead of a 'lying-in' home." In the article, Crutcher summarizes the "salient facets" of the proposal, treating it as if it were already almost a *fait accompli:*

> The University of Kentucky Medical Center is something more than a place to train doctors, nurses and dentists. One of its primary aims is to bring the fullest, and most modern, health care to all of Kentucky.
>
> . . . The University Center can, and will, provide at least four specialists to Morehead—internal medicine, pathology, surgery and radiology.

These four specialists will be full-time resident physicians at St. Claire, but will teach one day each week at the Lexington center. They will be on the U.K. staff.

. . . The specialists will handle cases referred to them by physicians. This means, in a broad sense, from general practitioners in this area of Kentucky.

. . . A salary of $15,000 a year for each of the four specialists . . . was discussed as the probable contract.

Northeast Kentucky Hospital Foundation . . . would underwrite the annual salaries.

All fees and charges by the four specialists would revert to the Northeast Kentucky Hospital Foundation.

. . . It is conclusive from other places where the plan has worked successfully [this apparently refers not only to Hunterdon but to Cooperstown, New York, which had developed a somewhat different administrative structure, though it was affiliated in a similar way with a university medical center and its specialists were indeed on salary] that charges made by the four specialists will meet their salaries with the possible exception of the first year . . .

Given such a plan (one that apparently reflected a tendency in medicine in the early 1960s, that decade which soon was to advance many other alarmingly idealistic causes), it is no wonder that the medical associations, as well as individual specialists, would want to disrupt it. While the relationship with the University of Kentucky Medical Center was to remain, the more controversial aspects of the Hunterdon plan lasted barely two years— the only defeat that I know of for Louise in her entire medical career, and one that, when it came, she accepted without bitterness and, indeed, with considerable grace, as if it constituted an inevitable compromise with the ideal in this, our imperfect human world.

10

In the years after Dr. Pellegrino left Hunterdon, the plan there underwent some drastic compromises, much as it did in Morehead. In both cases, the medical associations were in fierce opposition to a system in which physicians received salaries and thus were unable to determine their own fees and profits. Pellegrino said that even during his tenure at Hunterdon, "members of the medical community and organized medicine accused the staff of unethical practices because we were willing to accept salaries. They thought we were exposing ourselves to exploitation. It's interesting that none of us felt exploited."

A similar attack on the Northeast Kentucky Hospital Foundation, the employers of the doctors there, came from the Kentucky Medical Association; it was her speech to that group that Louise admitted she had bungled, chiefly from her belief that the virtues of the plan were so self-evident that she needed no rhetorical gift or strategy to persuade other members of her profession of its merits. She told me she received a letter from the KMA cautioning her against "government medicine,"

apparently a reference to the link between St. Claire
Medical Center and the University of Kentucky, and
another from the Kentucky Academy of General Practice warning her of "the dangers of socialized medicine."

Of course I wanted to see those letters, but neither
Louise nor Susie knew where they were, or cared to
look for them. "They were snotty," Louise said. "They
made me mad every time I saw them"; and Susie said,
"They were just awful."

As Louise and Pellegrino separately pointed out to
me, the present-day attitudes of medical associations are
less rigid regarding salaries than they were in the
1960s. Hospitals and other groups now routinely em-
ploy salaried specialists—for example, anesthesiologists,
pathologists, radiologists, and emergency-room physicians—without opposition from the medical societies.
But the opposition of those societies to this major aspect
of the plan in Hunterdon and Morehead carried serious
consequences for both hospitals. Concerning his Hunterdon experience, Pellegrino admitted that "the threat
distressed us," explaining that, for example, the attitudes of organized medicine "could have negative
effects so far as referring physicians [to us] were concerned." He believes that it was Hunterdon's very "success with patients that engendered the invidious
allegations of exploitation." Too (as seems apparent to
me from the difficulties with the plan at Morehead), the
position of the medical societies was advantageous to

individual specialists who for reasons of their own opposed a salary arrangement.

Pellegrino has written more than 350 articles and scientific papers, as well as a number of books and monographs, some of them in collaboration with others. The titles of many of the articles and of a majority of the books—for example, *Humanism and the Physician* (1979), *A Philosophical Basis of Medical Practice: Toward a Philosophy and Ethic of the Healing Professions* (1981), and *For the Patient's Good: The Restoration of Beneficence in Health Care* (1987)—suggest his interest in connecting, or reconnecting, medicine with values that transcend economics. "I'm not a socialist," he told me, "but I believe in something beyond profit. We're in difficult straits in medicine today because profit is dominating the scene." In both his New Jersey and Kentucky experiences, "surgeons constituted those most insistent upon the profit motive. In any debate on the subject, the swing vote was usually in the hands of radiologists, anesthesiologists, and pathologists. On fiscal matters they occupied an intermediate position between the surgeons and [those in] the surgical specialties on the one hand, and the internists, pediatricians, general practitioners, and psychiatrists on the other."

Internal grumblings about the system that converted medical specialists into salaried employees had occurred at Hunterdon while Pellegrino was medical director. "The ophthalmologist said, 'Ed, we have the best medical care I'm ever going to practice in my life, but I want to see the color of my money. I can't work this way.' I said, 'Fine, you have my benediction,' and I replaced him within a month; you have to let them go, when they don't find that way suitable to their interests. . . . The program was wonderful, we never had difficulty in getting young people to come. But you have to get people who are interested in medicine and patient care. Greed and selfishness, I think, brought the program down."

People, including those on hospital boards, "let doctors intimidate them," Pellegrino thinks. At Hunterdon, the salary system collapsed after his departure because "the board members lost their courage" when the radiologists wanted to "remain full-time and draw their salary and still have a radiology unit across the street from the hospital," a demand that was in violation of their signed contract. "The board of trustees didn't want to take them to court, didn't have the resolution."

At St. Claire Medical Center, the problems with the plan surfaced at the very beginning, for the chief of surgery at the University of Kentucky Medical Center refused to send surgical interns to Morehead. According to Louise, he "thought the interns shouldn't practice in any way except under him." Pellegrino "just couldn't understand why the Sam Hill" the surgical department at the University of Kentucky Medical Center wouldn't participate. "He held a board meeting and tried his best to explain," she said, but it wasn't until major changes in the Hunterdon plan were made at Morehead that surgical interns were permitted to come.

The impasse over those interns also brought about the withdrawal of Segnitz, who, according to Louise, had done "more than anybody else in getting the hospital set up." Discouraged by the lack of surgical interns, Segnitz decided against becoming director of the new hospital and, shortly before St. Claire opened, also withdrew his offer to serve as chief of surgery. (In our telephone conversation, he told me he had decided he could be of more help to St. Claire by staying at the University of Kentucky Medical Center, where he might be able to work from within to convince the chief of surgery there to supply interns to Morehead; too, he was disappointed that a friend, an internist whose skills he admired and whom he had hoped would join him at the new hospital, had declined the offer.)

Segnitz, though, worked to obtain a suitable replacement for himself as the initial director of St. Claire. Through his efforts and those of Willard and Pellegrino, Dr. Herbert Hudnut, an internist in residency at Mary Imogene Bassett Hospital in Cooperstown, New York (the hospital with some affinities with Hunterdon and Morehead), agreed to come as director and chief of medicine.

Hudnut stayed at St. Claire for only two years, but by the time he left, he had recruited several more specialists, the hospital was operating at capacity, and plans were under way to double the number of beds. Both

Hudnut and Louise were gratified by the success of the hospital's disaster plan in meeting its first major test. During the hospital's second year, a school bus slipped over an embankment, resulting in a number of major injuries. The hospital had practiced beforehand for such an emergency. "In eastern Kentucky, one sick or injured person is often accompanied by thirty relatives," Hudnut said, remembering the congestion at the hospital as part of the problem. "People came from all over to offer blood, to do whatever they could to help. We pinned notices on those who had been hurt, indicating their injuries and the need for X-rays. Warren Proudfoot [the chief of surgery] did a marvelous job of triaging, determining those we could treat at Morehead, those who had to be sent by ambulance to Lexington."

Hudnut had accepted the medical directorship at St. Claire because he liked the Hunterdon plan, which, among other virtues, had the built-in ability to circumvent the "sticky fingers" of specialists who wanted to hold on to their patients instead of sending them back to practitioners "like Dr. Louise." But the plan wasn't so advantageous to Louise as it might seem: "I think it must have been difficult for Louise and Susie when obstetrics was brought into the hospital," Hudnut said. "They already had a good system of care with their clinic. The new system was much less efficient for them; but they were willing, because of the overall benefits, to accommodate to the new concept. What a sparky person Louise is! She gets full credit for getting the hospital going."

During Hudnut's tenure, a greater problem than the lack of surgical interns came from the surgeons on the staff, who had a number of objections to the Hunterdon-type system, including the salary arrangement which gave them no preferment over the other specialists. The Northeast Kentucky Hospital Foundation made a small salary compromise in favor of the surgeons, but not enough to satisfy them. Hudnut, who "saw the writing on the wall," resigned as medical director and, shortly afterward, as chief of medicine. He left Morehead for the University of Rochester, to become assistant professor of medicine and assistant dean; in 1971, he began his private practice in Glens Falls, New York. (Since the imminent failure of a crucial aspect of the Hunterdon plan at St. Claire meant that he would have to revert to "the regular kind of practice," he decided he'd rather do that "regular practicing" in upstate New York.)

Several months after his departure, the St. Claire physicians severed their connection with the Northeast Kentucky Hospital Foundation. Judge Hogge, a board member of the foundation, said that specialists had been attracted to the hospital by the idealistic nature of the Hunterdonlike proposal, but became discouraged by the small number of patients they got. They felt that the few general practitioners who were practicing in the region weren't making sufficient referrals of their patients to them. Soon the surgeons and other specialists began to complain about further problems with the system. "It got so that it wasn't very pleasant," Hogge commented. "I remember one day they said that unless the system was changed they wouldn't operate further. It was what I would call a strike. We met with three or four doctors one morning for breakfast, and we had to surrender."

To Louise, the general practitioners weren't to blame for the failure of much of the program. "The surgeons didn't like to be paid the same amount as the internists, it was as simple as that," she told me. The "strike" occurred while she and Susie were vacationing in the Middle East. She continues to feel "a loss" that the scheme failed, but is philosophical about it—"What you believe, you can't make everybody else believe"—and she recognizes that St. Claire, operating under a more conventional policy (the specialists, fully separated from the Northeast Kentucky Hospital Foundation, have established two major clinics in town), has prospered, becoming a model for other areas. St. Claire remains a teaching hospital associated with the University of Kentucky Medical Center, as well as a hospital that has a cooperative arrangement with the general practitioners. "You find people coming here that have been in the big places," she said. "They say they can't understand a hospital like this in a town like this. I don't think there's a rural hospital anywhere that's any better."

The success of St. Claire Medical Center is summarized in an article written by Sister Mary Jeannette, its
administrator, and David Bolt, its assistant administrator of outreach service, in an article that appeared in the
September 1988 issue of *Health Progress,* the journal of
the Catholic Health Association of the United States.
(Pellegrino serves on its editorial board.) That article,
while mentioning the two major expansion programs
(in 1972 and 1980) that have raised the number of beds
from 41 to its current 170, finds that "the centerpiece of
St. Claire's development" is its home care and hospice
program, its outlying clinics, and its growth in specialty
services:

St. Claire, which had a medical staff of three in 1963,
now boasts a staff of 35 active physician members. In
addition, three of the five private practitioners in the
community have staff privileges. A majority of the medical staff is affiliated with the two multi-specialty group
practices in Morehead. Morehead Clinic, adjacent to the
hospital, has five internists, two obstetrician/gynecolo-
gists, a pediatrician, a pyschiatrist, an opthalmologist, a
family practitioner, and an oral surgeon in private practice. The Cave Run Clinic, a fourth of a mile from the
hospital, has two general surgeons, two vascular surgeons, three orthopedists, two urologists, a plastic surgeon, and a family practitioner. Other specialties are
available on a consultant basis at each of the clinics. These
include neurosurgery, dermatology, hematology/oncol-
ogy, and cardiology. A joint recruitment program

between the hospital and these two clinics targets up to 12 new physician specialists during the next year.

I have no way of knowing, of course, whether a hospital in a small town (according to the 1990 census figures, Morehead's population, excluding university students, is about 8,300, and the population of Rowan County slightly over 20,000) in the hills of eastern Kentucky could have attracted so many specialists without the dismemberment of that part of the original program that not only made salaried employees of its physicians but insisted upon equal salaries among those specialists. But given a whole society that typically equates freedom and the pursuit of happiness more with material than spiritual possibilities, it seems unlikely.

St. Claire continues to expand. A new obstetrics wing (a portrait of Louise by a local artist, Christine Barker, hangs there) was dedicated in the late spring of 1988, and a two-and-a-quarter-million-dollar cancer treatment center (a joint venture of the hospital and clinic physicians that will provide radiation therapy services) the following year. Though the 1989 recruitment goal was not quite met, by 1990 the staff of physicians had increased to forty-four, including specialists in nephrology and hematology/oncology. According to an article in the August 28, 1990, Morehead *News,* officials of the center are completing plans for yet another major expansion, which will include "a larger emergency room, an expanded radiology department, a new intensive care unit, and a new acute patient unit."

Susie may be "more adamant toward medicine today" than Louise considers herself to be, but she more openly concedes that it was "just as well" that the physicians are no longer salaried employees. Hudnut believes that St. Claire represents "a tremendous success story": the Hunterdon philosophy helped it to establish "high standards from the beginning," and—abetted by the continuing idealism and commitment of the "hardworking Sisters of Notre Dame," as well as a superb medical staff—it has maintained those standards.

Pellegrino, the instigator of the Hunterdon plan at Morehead, thinks that in general it is better to be defeated than to win victory through reprehensible means that appeal to the selfishness within all of us. He illustrated the point through a reference to a past presidential election: "Mondale said he'd raise taxes, and got clobbered; but he goes down with his reputation intact." But even Pellegrino sees the inevitability of some compromise. He told me, "Even with the failure of the ideal, Hunterdon and Morehead are better hospitals than they would have been," a fact that "fits my view: set the ideal high enough, and you end up with something better than you would have had otherwise."

Despite Louise's strictures against federal bureaucracy in health care, governmental programs have been important to the hospital in Morehead and its outreach programs. In their article in *Health Progress,* Sister Mary

Jeannette and David Bolt say that in the eleven counties of its primary service area, "unemployment ranges from 7 percent to more than 25 percent," the highest rate being in the "coal" counties of Appalachia, and that "medical assistance programs and Medicare are the largest insurers" of the patients treated. These administrators seem to have but one worry about the future of their hospital; they remark that "although St. Claire is a designated rural referral center for the Medicare program, future changes in the reimbursement formula, such as decreasing payment to rural hospitals, could be crucial."

Indeed, ominous signs are beginning to appear. Since the administrators wrote their article, a number of rural hospitals (much smaller ones than St. Claire, and apparently of the "lying-in" sort that Louise deplores) have closed because of a lowering of the reimbursement rate to rural facilities, which are considered cheaper to operate than their urban counterparts. Within the past year, I have read a number of newspaper accounts concerning the possibility of further cuts in Medicare assistance. According to one article, "the thrust of the approach [so far] has been to cut into the profits of providers such as hospitals rather than reducing benefits." Will such a tendency continue, threatening even hospitals like St. Claire with bankruptcy? One official of the federal government's Health Care Financing Administration thinks that the next round of cost-cutting will not affect hospitals; rather, he believes that "the next target will be doctor fees and that the outcry will be intense."

The Kennedy Institute of Ethics is only a short distance from the nation's Capitol, and *its* director, who has had considerable experience in such matters, would be one person for the government agency to consult; another would be a doctor in a small town in eastern Kentucky. Her sign may be gone from her clinic, but federal officials could ask anybody in town where to find Dr. Louise and get the directions at once.

11

During my years at Morehead, the college song was based on the tune of "I Wonder as I Wander," which, according to a local rumor, John Jacob Niles had first heard at the bus station in town, while listening to the blind ballad singer. Apparently the source of that rumor was Niles himself, for he wanted the ballad to seem a genuine folk song; actually, as he later confessed, it was his own composition. Whatever its genesis, the melody is a lovely one, the words appropriate enough to the isolation and religiosity of Rowan County's past culture. Though I then knew little of that culture, I was aware, as I have indicated, of a local sensitivity to some aspects of it, its provincialism as well as its propensity toward violence, and assumed that such a sensitivity underlay the college's attempt to replace the melody of "I Wonder as I Wander" with that of "High Above Cayuga's Waters," the song of the university I was to desert Morehead for. Fortunately, a competition for appropriate words to accompany that tune produced nothing suitable and the proposal was dropped.

That it ever had been made—by people who believed in the authenticity of the ballad they would replace— must seem quaint, if not incomprehensible, to the curator of Appalachian materials at the Morehead State University library and the majority of the faculty, as well as most of the present-day residents of the community. Morehead's insularity is now quite gone, and all defensiveness toward what once was. (Blind ballad singers are gone, too, not only because the old culture was connected with the insularity, but because cases of blindness—that handicap, once almost endemic to the region, which strengthens the voices of memory—have sharply declined, perhaps through dietary improvements as well as medical advances.)

Though I have stressed Cora Stewart and Louise Caudill, a history of the spiritual and material changes that have marked Rowan County since the days of Craig Tolliver's brutal despotism would have to include the activities of even more people than the ones I have referred to in this account. Many federal and state programs developed from the legacies of individuals like these. But especially in the years since I left Morehead, governmental programs have played an increasing role.

County roads have improved remarkably since the days that Cora Stewart initiated a secondary campaign to improve them. Federal funds, of course, paid for the construction of Interstate 64, which, connecting Morehead not only to Ashland and Lexington but to the whole network of similar highways spanning the nation, ended the isolation of the region in a way the railroad tracks never had. In addition, the Army Corps of Engineers' dam on the Licking River has increased the recreational facilities, bringing thousands of outsiders to the county for swimming, boating, fishing, and camping at Cave Run State Park.

While Medicare and other federal assistance plans have provided much of the hospital's income, permitting its growth, the state has subsidized the transformation of the small college I knew into the university it has become. According to an account in the Morehead *News* of November 30, 1990, Morehead State University had a fall-term enrollment of 8,622 students, an increase of over fifty percent since 1985. (The college became a university in 1966, three years after St. Claire opened.) The graduate programs lead to a doctoral degree in education, and master's degrees in fields as diverse as business administration, studio art, health, English, communications, vocational education, biology, psychology, and sociology.

The growth of the university is intimately connected

with that of the hospital: the university provides cultural enhancements for physicians who might otherwise hesitate to move to such a small town, while the presence of a hospital is necessary to attract both a large student body and a capable faculty. The two institutions have an academic bond; the university's nursing program, which includes the licensing of registered nurses, uses St. Claire for clinical training.

Like St. Claire, the university has established branch locations—satellites—throughout eastern Kentucky and now embraces the regional history, customs, and traditions that it once had shunned. Not only has it moved "Little Brushy," the first rural schoolhouse in which Cora Wilson Stewart taught, to a prominent place on the campus, but according to a Morehead *News* article on October 14, 1988, the university theater department staged a production of "First Shots of Rage," described as "an original play depicting the Martin-Tolliver feud in Rowan County." The nine performances were staged "in the old Rowan County Courthouse, the site of the . . . incidents" that were being dramatized. And, on September 7, 1990, the premiere performance of "Miss Cora," a multimedia production based on the life of Cora Wilson Stewart, was staged in Button Auditorium.

12

Most of the acquaintances Jean and I acquired during our six years in Morehead have either died or left the area. Bob Day, our neighbor who ran the Oldsmobile agency (the building burned to the ground some years ago) died during the summer of 1988; his wife, Lorene, appointed to the college faculty shortly after my departure, died only weeks after her husband. (Bob's middle name, as I learned from his obituary, was Button, and his mother was a Proctor, the latter connecting him to Louise; possibly, then, he was related not only to the clergyman who founded the normal school as an antidote to violence but to two families—the Days and the Tollivers—involved in the feud.)

Other than Louise and Susie, the only people we knew at all well who remain in town are Wilhelm ("Wilek") and Regina ("Gisa") Exelbirt. Wilek, the older of the pair, recently celebrated his ninetieth birthday. A Jewish couple from Vienna, they had escaped the Nazis to find security in Morehead, where the erudite Wilhelm for decades served as a history professor. A lecture series at the university has been named in his honor, and in 1990 he was given a Founders Day award for his long service to the university. (The front page of the Morehead *News* for April 3 carries a large photograph of the acceptance of the award plaque by Gisa for her husband, who had been unable to attend. The caption says that Exelbirt, an authority on Slavic European history, has been described by author and fellow historian Alex Haley as "a national treasure.")

The little bungalow the Exelbirts purchased on West Second Street (it now abuts the St. Claire parking lot) obviously was of crucial importance to the security they found in Morehead. It was a place of much warm hospitality for their many friends; in the early 1950s, Jean and I often visited them in the evenings, listening to opera recordings from Wilek's extensive collection and eating Gisa's delicious Austrian pastries. Their generosity was such that, when we were getting ready to leave for upstate New York, they offered to mortgage their house in order to buy ours, which we hadn't been able to sell, so we would have the cash to complete the transaction for another in Ithaca. We refused, of course, but the memory of that offer has remained, a bond with our Morehead past.

On each of our returns to Morehead, Jean and I have gone out for lunch or dinner at the Holiday Inn with Wilek and Gisa and on each occasion have argued over which couple would pay the bill. At our most recent meal there, Wilek spoke of the loss he felt at Bob Bishop's decision to close the drugstore. Wilek, who is bent by arthritis and must use a cane, doesn't get out of the house much, but for years one of his weekly excursions was to go by taxi to the drugstore; he would buy the Sunday *New York Times,* look over the racks of magazines and paperback books, have a cup of coffee at the fountain, and chat with Bob and other customers. The drugstore, I suspect, serves Wilek as token for much that is gone.

At the first Holiday Inn dinner, he went into a disquisition with me, telling me how fortunate it had been for me, as a writer, that William the Conqueror had made a successful invasion of England in 1066, for one of the results of that invasion had been the mingling of Romance and Anglo-Saxon languages that made English the flexible instrument it has become, with a vocabulary far in excess of all other major languages. On the spot, he constructed a paragraph that used only words derived from the Anglo-Saxon, comparing it with a similar paragraph based on words of Latin origin. It was an agile performance, a *tour de force* that won the rapt attention of most of the diners in the room, since Wilek's high-pitched voice carries well, particularly when he is enthusiastic. On warm spring days when classroom windows were open, I used to hear that same lecturing voice wherever I might happen to be, walking across a campus that then was small. To hear it now, after the passage of so many years, gave me the same feeling of poignancy that the voices of Martin Bookspan and Pru Devin have given me, as I have listened to them in the decades after leaving Morehead and the spot of land that somehow brought in WQXR as if it were a local station. But Bookspan and Devin I knew only as voices on the ether. Back in Morehead, I was glad to be sitting with Jean at a table in the restaurant of the Holiday Inn, located near the Interstate 64 inter-

change, with our old friends Wilek and Gisa there
before us, noble presences still.

13

In February 1988, Jean and I received a letter from Sister
Mary Jeannette, the administrator of St. Claire Medical
Center, whom we had met the previous year in Morehead while collecting information about Dr. Louise and
the hospital named for her as well as for the actual Saint
Claire. (Sister Mary Borromeo, the head of the Catholic
order at the same time that the Sisters of Notre Dame
agreed to run the hospital, was the one who suggested
St. Claire as a name that would encompass both
women.) The letter invited us to attend a community
celebration, on May 13, of "Dr. Louise Caudill's forty
years of practice and colorful life." It was to be one of a
number of events that St. Claire Medical Center was
planning for the twenty-fifth anniversary year of the
hospital's opening in July 1963. The program honoring
Dr. Louise would be held in Button Auditorium on the
Morehead State University campus, Sister Mary Jeannette wrote, and would include "school children and
friends portraying her early and professional life, music
by Jay Flippin's Combo and the Rowan County High
School Touring Choir, and dignitaries making presentations. Many of her 'babies' will be present that night."
    When Cris, our thirty-five-year-old son, learned that

we planned to attend, he said he wanted to accompany us: after all, he was the member of the family who had been born in Kentucky, and he had not been back since moving away at the age of three. Dr. Louise had not delivered him, for we had decided (as I have said) on a hospital birth—on the night he was to be born I had driven Jean the seventy miles of narrow and twisting blacktop to Lexington—but he wanted to meet the doctor who first took care of him, as well as to see the town where he had spent his earliest years.

Button Auditorium seats maybe a thousand people. In the early 1950s, college enrollment had been small enough so that all the students would fit into two-thirds of it for a weekly convocation that informally still carried its normal school title of "chapel."

On the night of the celebration for Dr. Louise, the crowd made the auditorium seem small, and unlike the students and faculty at the compulsory chapel, the audience was light-hearted and expectant. (Later I was to learn that originally the celebration had been planned as a surprise for Dr. Louise—a secret impossible to keep in a town as small as Morehead; and that when she learned it was to take place, she gave "doctor's orders" that it had to be "fun," without any long-winded testimonials.) Most of the seats in the hall were already taken, but Louise and Susie, who saw us as we made our way toward the front, made room for us in the rows that had been reserved for their relatives and the friends from Louise's Morehead public school days who still were living in the area—those whose childhood roles were to be assumed by Rowan County students in a series of skits.

The issue of the Morehead *News* that appeared the day of the celebration carried an illustrated two-page article about the experiences and achievements of both Louise and Susie and summarized some of the material that was to appear in the skits that evening. "No," the feature writer, Alice Akin, wrote, "the actors won't be professionals, but they will undoubtedly be playing to a friendly audience, a large section of which is likely to be made up of 'Dr. Louise babies.' And if only a fraction of the nearly 8,000 babies spanked into life by Dr. Louise show up for the celebration, it's reasonable to assume the applause will be ear-splitting."

J. D. Reeder, assistant principal of Rowan County High School, served as master of ceremonies, introducing the various skits (all of them written by Ellie Reser, a local resident and former nurse) and later the speakers who gave the brief testimonials. Rowan County Middle School children enacted scenes from Louise's early years, including a prank in which she, her sister Lucille, and other chums escorted a pony up the stairs of a friend's house and into the attic while the friend's parents were away. Older pupils played the parts of Louise and her high school companions: in that scene, "Louise" and "Bob Bishop" discussed their recent victory in a debate at another school, and "Bob" said that as usual he would be at Louise's house to study, after supper that night. Adults played Louise and Susie at the Oneida Maternity Hospital; in response to a question, "Susie" said with reluctance, "Yes, I think I'll try Morehead for a while," a remark that, given the longevity of the partnership between the two, brought applause, laughter, and cheers.

Next, Susie (known to several generations as the one who gave the injections) was the subject of a song performed by the high school touring choir; "If you knew Susie, like we know Susie (oh, ouch!), what a gal!" the choir sang. The final skit dramatized the visit of Monsignor Towell to Louise's clinic to ascertain if there truly existed a need for a hospital. For the sake of humor, but in accord with a Morehead legend that is a pardonable exaggeration, the skit enacted (if offstage, with the cries of the infants) the birthing of *six* children —two sets of twins and two other babies. At the conclusion of the skit, the actor playing Monsignor Towell made a telephone call to the head of the Sisters of Notre Dame in Covington to demand that the Sisters establish a hospital in Morehead at once. After listening to apparent objections, he declared into the phone, "If you can't say 'yes,' I'll have to call Rome," another line that brought laughter and long applause.

The skits ended and Reeder introduced Sister Mary Edwin, the first administrator of St. Claire Medical Center, along with other members of the Sisters of Notre Dame who had been part of the initial staff. The extended ovation they received testified to the affection and appreciation they had gained in the local community. Sister Mary Edwin, now in her mid-eighties, gave a brief speech. She spoke clearly, with a touch of a German accent and word order; she had come to America from Germany as a child. She said, "I can't tell you how happy we are to be here and to express our gratitude . . ." Here she looked over her spectacles to find Dr. Louise in the audience. "Dr. Louise," she said, "it took fifteen years for your dream to become a reality. I remember so well the day of the dedication of the hospital, and you were so very happy and you said to me, 'Sister, I think we have the most beautiful hospital in Kentucky.' Well, this little hospital has become now a large and important medical area center in the state of Kentucky. But really, for what are we so grateful to you, Dr. Louise? I think it is because of the forty years of service you have given to the medical profession and the healing profession. Nobody knows how many patients you treated with your love, with your help, and with your comfort. I don't know how many babies you have delivered, they say about eight thousand, how many people you have helped from dying. And for these services, Dr. Louise, we thank you, and we shall ask the good God to continue you here for many years to come."

The president of Morehead State University, C. Nelson Grote, spoke of Louise's service to his own family —she had been the family physician since 1960, and had delivered their two sons—as well as to the whole com-

munity. "Her contributions," he said, "can be measured in the qualities of the lives of all of us."

Proclamations and resolutions followed. Jack Roe,
the mayor of Morehead, and Ott Caldwell, Rowan
County judge-executive, declared May 13 as Claire
Louise Caudill Day. A resolution by the Kentucky
House of Representatives honoring her achievements
was read to the audience. Then Louise was called to the
stage for the final presentations. A slender young black
woman, Joan Taylor, introduced as a representative of
the governor, came to the podium, and, with the much
smaller, white-haired Louise at her side, began her
address: "On behalf of Governor Wallace Wilkinson, it
is indeed a pleasure to join you tonight in honoring Dr.
C. Louise Caudill. When we stop to marvel at this Kentuckian's forty years of quality medical and community
service, we think of all the people she has served and
the difference she has made in the lives of all who have
embraced both her wisdom and her love. Dr. Louise,
we love you, and we thank you for your dedicated,
selfless effort to enhance the quality of life for your
fellow Kentuckians, and in appreciation Governor
Wilkinson has issued the following proclamation on
behalf of the Commonwealth of Kentucky."

Here Joan Taylor read a proclamation that extended
"Louise Caudill Day" throughout the Commonwealth.
In referring to Dr. Louise's accomplishments, the proclamation mentioned that her "dedication took her up
the hollows and over the hills by bicycle or with horse

and wagon to deliver over two thousand babies in private homes in her earlier years, and in later years [she] delivered thousands more in medical facilities." This sentence drew laughter from the audience for its reference to Louise on a bicycle, since nobody had ever seen her traversing her rural rounds on one, her heavy medical bags and portable maternity table somehow strapped to her back. It was the only error in an eloquent statement, which drew a long ovation. At this point, if my recollection of the events is accurate, Louise began to clench and unclench a fist, as if she were embarrassed and wished to be elsewhere doing something useful, like sewing up a child's lip or encouraging a woman to push her baby from the womb.

But the governor's representative wasn't through; she read another citation from him giving Louise "the Governor's Outstanding Kentuckian Award," and then Miss Taylor announced that Governor Wilkinson had bestowed upon Louise yet *another* honor—the title that Kentucky governors freely, and not without humor, grant to those who have met their favor, that of Kentucky Colonel. This announcement produced perhaps the greatest laughter of the night.

After the portrait was unveiled, Reeder told the audience, "If Louise had chosen the traditional life and had had her own family, she might have reared a dozen children at most, but instead she chose a life of service to this entire community, and has birthed thousands of babies, nurtured hundreds of families through their illnesses and recoveries and has stood by all of us in times of death and grief." Then, as Jay Flippin's Combo struck up the melody "We Are the World," and the Rowan County High School Touring Choir sang a refrain that had been altered to make the words more applicable to the occasion ("We are the ones you brought into the world/And all the ones you've cared for . . . "), several hundred men and women, young and middleaged, all of whom had been delivered by Dr. Louise, proceeded down the aisles. While they were walking across the stage to shake her hand, Cris whispered to Jean and me, "If you hadn't gone to Lexington, I could be up there too." Overwhelmed by the emotion of the occasion, Jean and I wished he were.

Leaving the auditorium, I noticed that everybody was smiling. I was too, nodding and smiling at people I'd never seen before. It was the first time I'd attended an event in which I had become one with everybody there—actors, speakers, audience. Could a community elsewhere in the nation have come together in such spiritual cohesion to applaud one of its own? I thought about that question later, and supposed it likely, wherever a person like Dr. Louise has spent a professional lifetime.

A RAINSTORM

The following morning, Jean, Cris, and I attended a breakfast at the Holiday Inn for the out-of-town relatives and friends of Louise and Susie who had come for the celebration; we joined the same group that afternoon for a picnic on the terrace above Louise's tennis court. The sky was cloudless, the air mild and so clear that every tree and flowering azalea and even the most distant hill had its own sharp definition. In Morehead, Louise said, the entire spring season had been lovely like that, but the farmers said they needed rain. That kind of weather accompanied us all the way back to Ithaca on Monday. Wanting to prolong a happiness the three of us felt, Cris devised a homeward route that took us over or in view of seven covered bridges in southern Pennsylvania.

The sun predominated all that summer, accompanied by ever-growing heat and temperature inversions that occasionally turned it into a greenish orb; for smog from elsewhere can settle even over the rolling pastures of the Finger Lakes district. Drought conditions were far less apparent at my farmhouse, though, than they were elsewhere in the nation and throughout much of Europe, as well as (once again) in those regions of

Africa long familiar with the grief and hopelessness such conditions can bring.

In that community celebration, I felt I had been granted an emotional finale for my as yet mainly unwritten book, an event that I could use to mark both the end of a personal journey and the extent of a community's spiritual progress since Craig Tolliver had terrorized it. But the mass of material I had assembled—books, pamphlets, newspapers, tapes to be transcribed, pages of notes to decipher—was formidable. I listened to a tape of one of the interviews I'd made with Louise, enjoying as always the sound of her voice: the gentle irony, the sense of fun. Simply to listen to it permitted me to recapture a feeling for her spiritual essence, the quality that others, including me, responded to, as if through her they were recapturing something within themselves they had forgotten about. In the attempt to solve human problems that often seem intractable, Louise had told me, I remembered, "You just do one little thing after another"; and she had said, "If it's a help, especially to the little kids, it makes you a better person."

She had come to me in a dream as a kind of antidote to my sense of a human world becoming unreal and this was what she had told me. I felt like a little kid, myself. For the first time in my life I was beginning to see that my own sense of "reality," of whatever gave substance to human affairs, was a moral construction, one that required some possibility of goodness; without that possibility, the world was phantasmagorical.

In June, I watched the hummingbirds drawing nectar from the mock orange and honeysuckle blossoms in our front yard and listened to the bullfrogs recently come to our pond, their diesel-locomotive blare drowning out the rubber-band twang of their long-established smaller brethren. In July I watched the changing patterns of cumulus clouds that never gathered together in sufficient bulk to produce more than sporadic flares and a spattering of heavy drops in the dust, never a drenching rain, and saw the swallows darting just above the grass to catch insects and the hawks floating in the thermals high above us all. I watched and listened to these manifestations of the natural world that were oblivious to my anxieties, indifferent to anything I felt or believed, and wondered if I trusted myself and my species enough (look at the horrors and depravities we commit!) to tell a story of human goodness that, in transforming a tiny Kentucky county, had implications for us all.

Meanwhile, I was doing one little thing after another: transcribing the tapes, completing some onerous obligations that had nothing whatsoever to do with Louise or Rowan County. To the best of my knowledge, Louise (unlike me) had never known despair. Maybe, I thought, the real opponent of good isn't evil, but despair—the meaninglessness we feel when we doubt the presence or efficacy of that good. Some-

thing, some buried insight, kept eluding my conscious
mind.

August finally arrived. Halfway through that month,
Jean and I prepared for our customary vacation in the
Adirondacks. I lashed the two canoes to the car roof
(the larger one for carrying our food and camping
equipment to a suitable base camp, the lightweight
smaller one for portaging between mountain lakes). As
he had on the trip to Kentucky in May, Cris accompanied us. We elected to return to an island on Long
Pond in the St. Regis canoeing area that we'd stayed at
several years before; in the interval, the park service had
installed both a privy and picnic table, twin intrusions
of civilization upon a wilderness area that we didn't
mind.

We used the lightweight canoe for a number of portaging explorations we hadn't been able to make before.
The days were hotter than any we'd experienced in the
Adirondacks, but the nights were cool. After dark,
seated before the picnic table and within the pool of
light made by our gasoline lantern, we played rummy
and sipped wine while listening to the cries of the pair
of loons on the pond, whose presence meant that fish
were still to be found there, that the clarity of the water
wasn't a consequence (as it can be in the Adirondacks)
of its deadness from acid rain. My anxieties began to
thin out and disperse, much like the cloud of black flies
that pursued our speeding canoe the only time we had

been unwise enough to head for a wilderness area in June without an adequate supply of insect repellent.

One night I sat on a rock by the shore after Jean and Cris had gone to their tents; I was at once too tranquil and too alert to go to sleep, a condition that sometimes comes to me on camping trips just before a major change in the weather. Everything was still except for the cry of the loons; the stars were mirrored without distortion on the surface of the water. I said to myself, "If the soul is memory's desire, why then I have a soul," without understanding what I could possibly mean.

The following day was humid and overcast. Long Pond stretches for two miles or more. In the afternoon, we were paddling back from its farthest extent, Cris in the lightweight canoe and Jean and I in the larger and heavier one, when, unaccompanied by even a single clap of thunder, the weather changed. The temperature dropped, the rain descended. It was the storm whose intensity and size foretold the end of the drought in most of the eastern sections of the nation; the rain fell so heavily it threatened for a time to swamp both canoes, for we'd brought no bails.

That rain blurred my vision, making the canoe a microcosm I shared with my wife. Looking over my shoulder, shielding my eyes with a hand, I saw the microcosm in which Cris moved as a vague oblong. In advance of our canoe swam the pair of loons, who seemed to have taken on the task of guiding us home—

they had preceded us ever since we had started back, diving beneath the water whenever we came too close. "Now I know what it feels like to be a loon," I cried to Jean above the sound of the downpour. She laughed and, mimicking a famous sentence by a Swedish movie actress, cried back, "I vant to be a loon!" Sealed in by the hills and clouds and shimmering sheets of rain, the pond itself was a microcosm containing two loons, three people in two canoes, and a myriad of fish beneath the surface. Was it raining like this on the pavements of New York City, on the corn and oat fields of the Finger Lakes, on the forested hills of Rowan County, Kentucky? Each was a microcosm within another microcosm—the tiny globe bearing its freight of children (humans and loons alike) that was sailing with its barren siblings and radiant parent through the dry seas that are the immensity of space; and at the instant I felt that kind of communion I felt also how incredible and how perverse it was that I or anybody else could wonder what goodness was, or doubt its presence within our species.

Probably all revelations have long been secretly rehearsed and are guided by memory. They arrive within us as a feeling we instantaneously recognize as true. In the next moment, they begin to take on the shape of an extended and unified thought whose elements all along had been waiting in the memory for a propitious moment of release. In my case, the thought began with the sentence that had come to me the night before. To it, my memory added some personal experiences that had been abetted by some reading I'd done. As best I can communicate it today, my thought went something like this:

If the soul is memory's desire, why then I have a soul; and what it wants more than anything else is that unobtainable happiness in which pure freedom is to be found —freedom from consciousness, from the prison of my ego, from my impurities, from my own banal self; freedom to return to its beginnings in the natural world, perhaps to its origin in the uncaring cosmos itself. Chekhov, the writer I would emulate if I could, recognized this desire for an impossible freedom as a human constant, as the happiness for which we are all in search, and from such insight came not only his objectivity but his compassion and implicit morality. Human life remains a mystery our reason can't penetrate, but moral choices do exist: what is good increases the possibilities of freedom and happiness for others as well as ourselves, being actions that alleviate suffering, ignorance, and social injustice; what is evil consciously restricts or cancels those possibilities and takes on the names that make us banal. The soul that wants release from the human world is inexorably drawn back to it—in compassion, yes, but also to savor the degree of good and unity to be found there—as mine had been through a dream in which my memory saw my wounded son and Dr. Louise's trembling hand.

In writing this paragraph now, long after that rainstorm, I have been aided by a smudged and barely deci-

238

pherable note that I put on a damp sheet of paper soon after the three of us reached our camp, changed our clothes, and were sitting under the canopy we'd attached to trees so that it would shelter our picnic table. I was trying to hold on to the feeling for whatever it could offer me and the project I now wanted to get back to. Mine had been a reaffirmation that came as a revelation, I supposed, simply because I had sensed it for the first time as the truth of my own drenched body. On that sheet of paper I jotted down a long-familiar sentence from an otherwise forgotten book: "Memory is what we now have in place of religion." But we always have had that—before religion (that institutionalization of a preexistent spiritual impulse), before words with their seemingly infinite regress.

What had happened to me on the pond was little more than an old acknowledgment that I belonged to the natural world from which I had come. Recognizing that, I also realized that I could trust my memory for the other things it knew.

===

By early winter, I was nearing the completion of the first draft of this book. The December issue of my favorite magazine, *Natural History,* contained its regular column by Stephen Jay Gould, that Harvard biologist, paleontologist, historian of science, and engaging essayist who for years has been following the various channels of his bliss, one of them being further evidence to document the validity of his "punctuated equilibrium" theory of evolution. The basic nature of the human animal has been unchanged since it first was shaped, he says, and that nature is predisposed toward kindness, a fact that can be statistically demonstrated. The tragedy of our species lies in "a cruel cultural asymmetry" that permits the rare event—the eruption of meanness—to constitute our admittedly dark history. In other words, one evil act can topple ten thousand good ones.

But history has yet to extinguish us, and common goodness eventually may prevail over meanness to form a new chronicle of events, as I believe has already happened—at least for this moment in time—in Rowan County, Kentucky. Soon after the community celebration in May, Louise and Susie left for a leisurely Alaskan cruise; by December they had been back at work for a long time, doctoring their eastern Kentucky friends, something they're still doing today.

ACKNOWLEDGMENTS

I have depended on too many sources for the material in this book to acknowledge them all. I would like to thank those people of Morehead, Kentucky, many of them friends and patients of Dr. C. Louise Caudill and her nurse Susan Halbleib, who gave me information and anecdotes about them and the community. I owe a particular indebtedness to Jack Ellis, former director of the Morehead State University library, for the extensive documents he lent me, some on the Rowan County War and others on Cora Wilson Stewart. For the chapters about St. Claire Medical Center, I received considerable assistance from Dr. Edmund Pellegrino, director of the Kennedy Institute of Ethics and professor of medicine and medical humanities at Georgetown University in Washington, D.C.; Dr. Herbert Hudnut, Jr., a Glens Falls, N.Y., internist; Dr. Richard Segnitz, a Public Health Service physician in Culbertson, Montana; and Judge Elijah M. Hogge, a lifelong resident of Morehead, and his wife, Norma.

I am indebted to the University of Kentucky library and to Willie Everette Nelms, Jr., whose exemplary 1973 master's thesis, *Cora Wilson Stewart: Crusader*

241

against Illiteracy was (along with Mrs. Stewart's own *Moonlight Schools*) a major aid to my understanding of that woman's accomplishments.

But my major indebtedness is to Dr. Louise and Susie, for being who they are, as well as for putting up with all my questions.

Quotations from Nelms's thesis and the following sources are gratefully acknowledged:

Let Us Now Praise Famous Men, by James Agee and Walker Evans, copyright 1960 by Walker Evans, published by Houghton Mifflin Co.

The Power of Myth, by Joseph Campbell with Bill Moyers, copyright 1988 by Apostrophe S Productions and Alfred van der Marck Editions, published by Doubleday.

Night Comes to the Cumberlands, by Harry M. Caudill, copyright 1962, 1963 by Harry M. Caudill, an Atlantic Monthly Press book published by Little, Brown and Co.

Little Kingdoms: The Counties of Kentucky, 1850–1891, by Robert M. Ireland, copyright 1977 and published by the University Press of Kentucky.

"A Success Story in Kentucky," by Sister Mary Jeannette, S.N.D., and David Bolt, in *Health Progress* for September 1988 (vol. 69, no. 7), copyright 1988 by the Catholic Health Association of the United States.

Kentucky: Decades of Discord, 1865–1900, by Hambleton Tapp and James C. Klotter, copyright 1977 by the Kentucky Historical Society.